Adoption Matters

Orphan Train to Modern Day
Nonfiction Short Stories of Adoption
& Foster Care

Dianne L. Rowe

ADOPTION MATTERS:
ORPHAN TRAIN TO MODERN DAY
NONFICTION SHORT STORIES
OF ADOPTION & FOSTER CARE

Dianne L. Rowe

17459 90th Avenue North
Maple Grove, MN 55311

Book Layout ©2017 BookDesignTemplates.com

Adoption Matters/ Dianne L. Rowe. —1st ed.

Compiled by Carolyn Wilhelm

Cover image from Pixabay.com

Photos by Authors

ISBN (p) 978-0-578-61524-0

Library of Congress Control Number:

2020901353

CONTENTS

An "Orphan Train Rider" From New York City 1

A Short History of the Orphan Trains 5

Adoption Matters 9

Twelve Years and Counting 21

My Adoption Story 33

Ninety Years Young and Finding Family 39

Stephanie and Her Friends, Who Are Family .. 45

A Precious Gift 49

Untitled 57

The Most Wonderful Phone Call 59

A Boy Is 67

Meeting Shin Hyun Ok 69

My Adoption Story 77

She Had Me at Umma 95

Melanie's Story 103

Coping with Identity Problems 109

The Accident 119

Patti 125

Meant to Be 131

A Baby Is A Miracle 143

A German Girl in Our Lives 145

No Longer the Eldest..165

There is a Song 171

About the Authors 173

Lois Miller Caswell..175

Katie DeCosse..177

Esther and John Holgate 178

Ann Kalin 181

Christopher Luehr 183

Jackie Maher 185

Dawn McClean 187

Dianne L. Rowe 188

Irene Reuteler..189

Mary (Marge) Smith..190

John Strahan..192

E. Irene Theis...194

Leif Wallin 195

Carolyn Wilhelm..196

David Zander 197

God's Reason 199

Thank you for Reading! 200

Footnotes for A Short History of Orphan Trains

....201

*Dedicated in memory to my wonderful role-model my mother, who taught
and showed me compassion, how to be a strong woman, and yet loving.
And to all the mothers in our stories.
Your precious gifts have been received
with much gratitude and love.
And love... will always find a way!*

Dianne

"Ask and it will be given to you; seek

And you will find; knock and the door

will be opened to you. For everyone who

asks receives; the one who seeks finds; and

to the one who knocks, the door will be
opened."

Matthew 7, Verse 7-8

CHAPTER 1

An "Orphan Train Rider" From New York City

By Dianne L. Rowe

She was born in New York City in 1897 and was left at the New York Foundling Hospital when she was just a few days old. At the age of two, she was put on one of the Orphan Trains from New York and sent to a family in Little Falls, Minnesota. This was called "placing-out." Records were sloppy back then, and though she later tried to get information, it always ended with nothing of substance. Consequently, she knew very little about herself. We did learn she was brought to the home and put in a crib by the front door of the Foundling Hospital, where babies were often left.

Her name was Frances.

FRANCES 4- OR 5-YEARS OLD

The priest from a Church in North Prairie had announced that there would be an orphan train arriving with children if anyone wanted (*or needed)* a child. He asked that they sign up. There was a family who put their name in for a boy and a girl. When the day came for the children to arrive, many people came to watch and to pick up children. Among them was the woman who had signed up for two children. The boy she signed for was four years old and the girl, Frances, was two. When the woman saw two-year-old Frances, she said she couldn't bring this child home because she was too frail, and her husband would be angry, so she took the boy and left Frances. Another woman was at the train, herself being the mother to fourteen children, many of them grown. When she saw that this woman had rejected Frances, she said she wanted her, so she took her home to the farm. Frances was treated well even though they didn't show much affection. Her mother was lively and fun, while her father was quite religious with little humor.

In the summer by the age of eight, Frances would leave home at 6:00 a.m. with the herd of cows and not return until 6:00 p.m. – when she heard the six o'clock church bells ringing.

At the age of 13 her father died and life changed. Her brother had inherited the farm and he and his wife moved in. For a short time, Frances and her mother lived in the home but, eventually, Frances was asked to leave. The wife did not feel she wanted to feed the mother and Frances too. Now only thirteen years old,

Frances set out alone to make her own life as best she could and her education stopped...at 8th grade.

She found work in Little Falls at a hotel doing laundry. Other times, when she ran out of work, she would knock on doors and ask if they needed help. When she found work in their homes – she would do their cooking, baking, helping care for their children whatever was needed. On days off, she traveled by train to her sister's home in Holding Fort, Minnesota, where she helped with her sister's large family.

Frances survived and matured into a lovely, capable, and independent woman. At 17 years, she married and raised nine very responsible children with her husband who loved and cherished her for 49 years till his death.

She was a woman before her times as she worked both in the home and out of the home, but it was her family and home that always meant everything to her. At 98 years young, she passed away. Frances Wodarck was my mother – an amazing woman.

CHAPTER 2

A Short History of the Orphan Trains

By Dianne L. Rowe

The Orphan Trains of New York is a historical event in the history of our country which has received little attention even though it has affected over two hundred thousand people in the United States.[1]

It began around 1854[2] in, the City of New York. Poverty was mounting. Industry and urbanization were growing. Families were torn apart, with children being the greatest victims. The population of children was overwhelming in New York with little or no guidance. Public school was not yet mandatory[3] and, consequently, serious crimes among children were out of control.

In 1853, the **Children's Aid Society** was founded[4] and steps to help the children began. The Society proposed education, employment, religious training and industrial training; however, the greatest problem was that the children needed homes. It was believed that the children would be better off outside of New York in homes in the country...where the farmers needed help and the children could help. This process was called ***placing-out.***

Placing-out is labor in return for a room and education.[5] This was favored because it left the door open if the arrangement didn't work out - either party was free to end the placement...so began the ***orphan trains***. The Children's Aid Society provided children of all ages up to 14 years.

The New York Foundling Hospital run by the Sisters of Charity[6] was also instrumental. They provided children between the ages of 1-4 years. These trains were called "Baby Specials" or "Mercy Trains." Potential parents applied to the Foundling and could request the age, gender or special features of the child they wanted.

Children were gathered from all over the city, scrubbed, dressed in clean clothes, and made to look presentable for their long ride.

The first train departed from New York on September 20, 1854, and headed for Detroit with 46 children aboard. Their ages were 7 to 15 years. Their arrival was a major event for the small communities, with the distribution of the children usually taking place in a church. A representative with the children would give a short speech about the work of the Society and shared information about each child.

For seventy-five years, the trains ran, the last one departing in 1929.[7] The trains brought these children to towns with hope for brighter tomorrows, and for some, it was brighter...but not for everyone.

CHAPTER 3

Adoption Matters

Not flesh of my flesh

Nor bone of my bone

But still, MIRACULOUSLY my own.

Never forget for a single minute,

You didn't grow under my heart,

But in it.

By Fleur Conkling Heyliger

A LITTLE BACKGROUND-

By Dianne L. Rowe

My husband and I were raised in large families. We knew the fun of having siblings. We also knew the disagreements and frustrations, but the pluses outweighed the minuses we thought, so having children was just part of our plan when we married.

In 1960 we married and five years later had our first child...not our plan to wait so long. Several years passed, and no second child. We now realized our second child might not happen, or it might be quite a wait again. So, we decided to be proactive and applied for adoption. We knew we could love a child that wasn't our biological child. We also knew that if we were fortunate enough to have a third child, that would be perfect, and it never mattered to us if we had a boy or a girl...we just wanted a baby.

The first part of the adoption process involved going to meetings along with other couples who were hoping to adopt too. For nine months, we met with a counselor who interviewed us, screened us, and visited our home. Once we were accepted, our preparations began...get the family baby crib, get diapers, bottles, and so on. And finally, the call came...our baby was born...***A Baby BOY!***

The day was warm and sunny as the three of us left our home in Golden Valley and headed to the Catholic Charities in downtown Minneapolis to meet our baby son and bring him home.

Before they let us see him, they dressed him in the clothes we had brought.

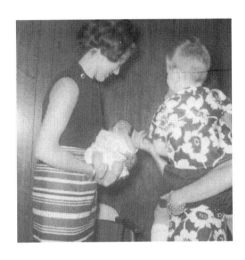

MRS. MOORE, THE SOCIAL WORKER

A DREAM COME TRUE!

Our Baby was adorable, so handsome, so alert, and so **very, very hungry...but not crying!** (I recognized a hungry baby.) Luckily, I had brought along a new sterilized pacifier, which he immediately took. **Yup! He indeed was meant to be our baby.**

When we got home, the first thing we did was feed our son his first bottle with us. He loved his bottle and felt wonderful in our arms. All three of us were delighted.

Baby, Michael, Dad & "First" Bottle

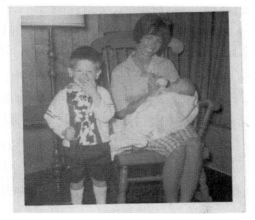

BABY, MICHAEL, MOM ...BOTTLE

Soon after our arrival home Michael, brought in some of his little friends to see his brother. One little boy, Tony, mentioned that they had gotten his brother from the hospital...I remember smiling and said, "Oh!"

By evening family members stopped by to welcome our new addition. Babies have a way of charming and attracting people - which he did.

THE EVENING VISITORS

Our baby would be called Robert, Rob (but not Bob). We thought his name suited him perfectly. It was a strong name that would carry him well in whatever field he would choose. The middle name was a bit of a struggle. After trying many names with Robert, we tried Patrick. It worked!

He was Irish - we had been told, so that was perfect...Robert Patrick Rowe.

Within a few weeks of Rob's arrival, we had his second baptism at St. Margaret Mary's Catholic Church in Golden Valley, MN. He had been baptized shortly after he was born, but this was his baptism with his family.

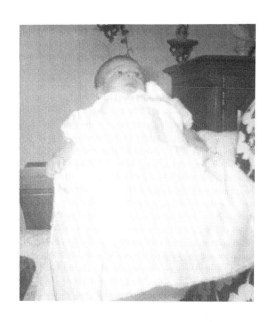

R O B E R T   P A T R I C K

Isn't he handsome?

He was such a fun and happy baby, not one bit crabby. He loved his bath and his jumper swing, but when he got a little older – he didn't enjoy the car ride. My remedy was to bring something along for him to eat (such as crackers and so on) to distract him.

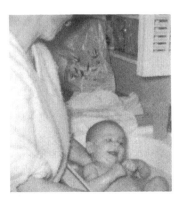

OUR HAPPY BABY!

He could really make that swing jump!

Rob was such a good baby. He took great naps and could fall asleep just about anywhere we were. For a while, he would wake up in the middle of the night...not crying but not sleeping.

I would hold him, and soon he would go back to sleep. One day I found a bunch of Cheerios in his crib. It seemed his brother was going to share his treat with him.

When he was two, he said his first big word. We were driving by one of the Honeywell plants, and I said, "There's Honeywell." And he said..."Honeywell." I couldn't believe what I heard. A three-syllable word as clear as could be for his first big word. (He's a genius!)

At the age of 4 years, he went to pre-school at the Baptist church three mornings a week with a couple of neighborhood children – Carma and Scott. I thought he might cry when I left him...but that never happened. He was ready!

Throughout all his schooling, including college, he was an excellent student, never procrastinated, always, self-disciplined.

In first grade, he shocked our family again as he learned to spell "PHOTOSYNTHESIS" for one of his spelling words that week.

(Our amazing genius!)

In grade school for a time, he would walk in the door after school and go right to the dining room table and do his homework...and be done in ten minutes.

(Who is this child???)

When Rob was two years, four months, we

had our third child – a little girl. Needless to say, he was not impressed, but his calm, easy-going personality seemed to accept her anyway.

We didn't make a big deal about his being adopted. When he was little, I would say things like, "The day we adopted you..." so he would know the word, and when he was older, I would say to him, "If you have any questions, I have answers." And I would try and get him to ask questions, but He never would. I remember there was a program on the television regarding adoption, so I had the two of us watch – thinking he would have questions, but no questions came.

With three children, life got a bit hectic, and somehow, I never got around to mentioning to Rob's little sister that he was adopted until she was five years old. So, one day, when she was home from school, and we were alone, I thought this is the moment. I sat her down and told her our wonderful story. I thought she would have questions, but all she said was, "Neat! Can I go out and play now?" At the time, I thought the questions would probably come later.

When Rob was an adult, married, and a parent, his biological parents, looked him up. They had married each other and had sent info to Catholic Charities regarding medical information...if he was interested. He contacted Catholic Charities and learned there was a letter and a picture from them. He also learned he had a biological sister who, at that time, was eight years old. They live out of state but keep in touch.

We have all met and they, like Rob, are wonderful, so it has been a good outcome. Our son now has all his questions (he never asked me) answered, and that was all I ever wanted for him. That he never has to wonder.

At Rob's college graduation from the University of Minnesota, I couldn't help but have a heavy, but a happy heart. I was so very proud of what he had accomplished and who he had become. I knew how hard he had worked to get his education - as he did it all by himself, ...working, and going to school. Even when he had to transfer out of state for a few years because of his job, he enrolled in that state's college and never missed a beat.

Rob brought so much to our lives. He was always interesting, adventurous, thoughtful, and caring. And he had an easy-going kind of temperament - that made him so easy to love.

Recently, he discovered there is an artistic side to him that no one ever knew existed. It just surfaced and is pretty exciting. He creates and makes beautiful water fountains, pictures of stone, messages on stones, etc. This has become his hobby and occupies any spare time he has.

Yes, indeed! Robert Patrick captured our hearts and is one of our greatest blessings. Does

Adoption Matter? We know that...

Adoption <u>truly</u> does matter!

CHAPTER 4

Twelve Years and Counting

By Jackie Maher

It is 2019, as I set about telling my story. It is also 12 years since, for only the second time in my life, I laid eyes on the young woman to whom I had given life fifty years before. I was a victim of the 1950's mentality toward unwed motherhood. We had committed the sin that was nearly unforgivable. The world said we were bad and we bought it. We deserved to be shunned - to be put out of our homes and schools and we had no one to blame but ourselves. That is what they said. And who were they? They were our parents, teachers, friends, clergy, and anyone else who felt it gave them a leg up in the pecking order. We only did what a lot of young people did but not did not get caught.

My support system was weak and ultimately lacking in empathy and understanding. My mother told me that I could not bring the baby home, not that I ever intended to. After all, "What would the neighbors say?" By this time, my mother had almost singlehandedly raised five children and the light at the end of the tunnel was getting closer and brighter, and her load was getting lighter.

At the time I was living in Minneapolis with three other girls. I was working full time and totally supported myself. In the 50's, women were expected to take leave of their jobs a few months into their pregnancy.

Ultimately, I turned to Catholic Charities for guidance and moral support. I entered the Catholic Infants Home just weeks before my baby, a girl, arrived. A small number of women were able to take their babies home with them. That solution was not available to me. Most of us were sent home with empty arms and told to forget and get on with our lives.

Did we really believe this was possible? We earnestly tried to forget. We came out of the home for unwed mothers and started to reclaim our identities. We pocketed our grief, took back our names, found new jobs and made new friends. We tried to gain back our respect for ourselves as well as the respect of others. We worked hard.

Before long I found a new job, a place to live and friends, some old and some new. I soon met the man I was to marry. We raised five beautiful children and in the vernacular of today, I redefined myself. Only twice in the following years did I ever discuss this time in my life and then only briefly. I jealously guarded my secret.

Meanwhile, years became decades, and somewhere along the way, the rules changed. Adoption became "open," and single parenthood was no longer an aberration. Unwed mother became an antiquated term. And somewhere there was a woman, someone's daughter, my daughter, perhaps an adoptee in search of her birth parent. Meanwhile as I raised my five other children, this daughter resided in the shadows of my memory, and as the song goes "ever gentle on my mind."

Then one day, my seventieth birthday passed and the loose ends of my life began clamoring for attention for resolution. I needed to put my identifiable information on record in case my daughter needed it. I also had to inform my other children of my long-kept secret. Finally, we could talk openly about the situation. And from some of them came, "WOW Mom that is so exciting."

Some were more cautious. But "exciting?" Where had I been? When had this happened? What about the shame? My concern was that I might not have many years left and what if I had answers that my daughter had been looking for? How was her health? Was she looking for genealogical roots? And might she be angry with me for waiting so long? And the worst-case scenario, had she already passed away? It was time for me to know, to give and receive answers to the questions that lay between us.

I expected that the search with its red tape and inhibiting laws would take at least months. I was lucky. I finally had a support system through friends and the help of Concerned United Birthparents. Within two weeks, I had enough information to make my approach. This is the letter (in part) that I sent Katie.

May 12, 2007

Dear Katie,

I am sure this letter is coming as a surprise to you. I recently initiated a private search to locate a daughter that I had surrendered for adoption in 1957. The search culminated in finding you. If you are wondering why I chose to search at this late date, let me just say that suddenly all of the obstacles fell away, and I found good people to advise me and help me in my search. My gratitude to them is eternal.

To better introduce myself, let me give you some information on my life today. My husband and I raised five children and a number of cats and dogs. We are both seventy-one years old and retired for the most part. He still maintains an interest in his chosen field of veterinary medicine. My interests include golf, reading, (I cannot pass a book store or a library), and have many books in my collection waiting to be read. I recently enrolled in a creative writing class and have been told my stuff is pretty good. I belong to three card clubs and enjoy outings with friends. My husband and I have done some extensive traveling over the years and I have discovered I also like traveling alone. I'm told that he travels fastest who travels alone. Suits me well.

Now I would like to know about your life if you see fit to have contact. I can perhaps answer any questions regarding health or genealogy. There is a lot of Irish in us. Perhaps we could meet over a cup of coffee or? It has been my prayer all these years that you have had a good and loving home. It is the wish of all birthmothers; I believe when we find that we are not able to keep our child. Would you please let me know soon whether you wish contact or not? Thank you for that.

I look forward to hearing from you. Take care,

Love,

Jackie

PS: I timed this letter so as not to impose on any

Mother's Day traditions you might be observing.

Katie's response in part.

May 14, 2007

Dear Jackie,

I thought it was all downhill now that my 50th birthday celebration is officially over. As is typical for me, I am in a fugue state between information and comprehension. It generally takes 12-18 hours for BIG news to sink in. However, I know you have been thinking of this for a lot longer than I have, so I won't keep you hanging. In fact, if you are like me, you want an answer now.

I have never seriously considered searching for you but have always been open to the prospect of meeting should you initiate it. Meanwhile, I will take this opportunity to tell you a little about myself.

I am currently the Clinical Training Coordinator, as well as an instructor in the Veterinary Technology program at Argosy University. My background in vet med is a degree from MIM, followed by 16 years as a veterinary technician in small animal clinics. I began my career in September of 2001, the eleventh to be exact

I live with my husband, dog, and cat and have two grown stepchildren with children of their own. For various reasons, I chose not to have children of my own, so alas no long-lost grandchildren. I have one older brother and one younger sister who were also adopted. My husband being 18 years older than I am has retired from his career as a Social Worker. Both of my parents are very creative, artistic people and that has lent itself to a very interesting life. I have had every advantage available in the way of education and opportunity.

I, too, cannot pass a book store and have several books waiting to be read. I also enjoy crafts; crocheting and silk flower arranging are my current favorites. I, too, enjoy writing and have been told I am quite good at it.

Anyway, that is me in a nutshell. I look forward to corresponding by email for now and am sure that at some point we will meet face to face. I look forward to our journey.

Katie

That journey continued beyond letter writing on May 27th, 2007. On a sunny May afternoon, we met in a park and after the first hugs and tears subsided, we spent several hours just talking and getting reacquainted. I didn't know if she wanted to see me again so I was going to make the most of it. Before we split up, she asked to meet again and unbeknownst to me, we were off and running.

It has been a journey indeed. We have laughed together, cried together and vacationed together. We spent time in CA., SC., AZ, FL, and Branson, MO. Yet none of these can hold a candle to our "week at the lake."

It was September of 2007 when we took a cabin at a lake near Pine River. We brought Katie's pet Cavalier along in case we needed a tension diffuser. We took several walks on *THE PAUL BUNYAN TRAIL. We* went for massages, shopped for candles and books, ate chocolate and watched movies. In the morning, we would bundle up for coffee on the porch. And after dark, Katie would start a bonfire, and we would sit outside in the chilly evening air and just talk. We kept a journal and recorded our thoughts and impressions, discovering our many things we had in common. It was the vacation that left me with the best memories of all our trips.

I wish all stories could unfold like ours but that is not meant to be. Some parents prefer to stay hidden. Some adoptees do not wish to be found. And in spite of everything, even our road has its bumps. A lot of lives have been affected. Family dynamics have changed in spite of the fact that we tried to keep this transition as smooth as possible.

Katie may weave in and out of my life as the others do. We knew early on that we could not capture those fifty years of separation but we have endeavored in these last twelve years to embrace this new relationship as fully as possible. We even ventured early on to put pen to paper and share our story with those who were experiencing or have experienced similar stories. In 2009 we chronicled this adventure in FIFTY YEARS IN 13 DAYS. We may have encouraged others to take this same step in spite of the risks involved. We worked hard to build a strong relationship. We have done well. This is the final closure.

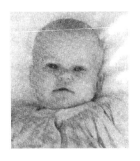

Katie, at two months old shortly after arriving at her new home.

Katie in elementary school.

Here she is in about 3rd grade.

Katie's love of animals knew no bounds.

"Bill, Katie, Jackie, and Don celebrating Katie receiving her Master's from Saint Mary's."

CHAPTER 5

My Adoption Story

By Katie DeCosse

This is my story. I was placed for adoption in 1957. Fifty years later my birthmother Jackie, found me and we were together once again. It wasn't until reunion that I was really able to look back on those many years and learn things about myself that I had never realized before. I think adoptees all have a different approach to life and how they handle the experience. Every journey is different, with no predicting how life will turn out.

The first fifty years, in a nutshell, went like this. I was raised in a Catholic household and attended parochial schools from 1st grade through college. We were a family of five, with all three children adopted as infants. My brother is two years older than I, and my sister was five years younger. My brother has lived his life as the "perfect" adoptee while my sister struggled her entire life to find peace. Although she had some mental health issues, I believe that she never got past the early rejection of her mother placing her for adoption. *But that is her story, not mine.*

For many years I was a veterinary technician, both in a clinic setting and later, as a veterinary technology instructor. I never had children, so my spare time was available to pursue my own interests. At this time in my life, I am married and we share our home with two dogs and a cat. Career-wise, I have completely switched gears and now work in the world of art and textiles.

I think all I ever wanted was fit in. While I couldn't put words to it as a child, there was always of a feeling of not really belonging. That carried into other parts of my life. My parents were quite strict so aside from being an adoptee. There were other times I felt that I didn't fit in. There were things other kids could do or have, that were denied me. As an adolescent, that was very hard at times. In hindsight of course, it wasn't that horrible but for a child trying to fit in it seemed to just add another layer of difference to an already fragile sense of inclusion.

The biggest thing I learned since reunion is also the most difficult to explain but I will try.

When a baby is born, they immediately know who Mom is and a connection is cemented. The child is then further validated as s/he grows up surrounded by people who share similar traits. I believe that is where a child learns a sense of self and a place in the world. This connection is so strong and yet goes unnoticed because it is just who they are. The adoptee doesn't experience this validation and, furthermore, doesn't really know what is missing. But something is.

I discovered this one evening when I was visiting with a new brother, one of Jackie's subsequent children. We were having a conversation and I had this eye-opening moment where it felt like we were tracking each other's thoughts and then verbalizing almost identical responses. This was very early on in our relationship so there was no way we could have known what the other would say. This experience went beyond simply being of the same opinion. It was quite profound.

My adoptive parents are both avid readers, and I am seldom without a book. Upon reunion, Jackie and I both discovered that we never pass a bookstore without stopping. That was an area where my innate love of reading intersected with the same interest in my parents. Jackie and I are both crocheters; that was not a part of my growing up years. Some parts of me surfaced even as I had no idea from where that interest was coming.

There are so many myths surrounding the world of adoption with each of the members of the triad having to deal with their own set of expectations. My family was not the perfect one that most people assume when they learn you are an adoptee. It was many years before I was able to honestly address that assumption. Adoption doesn't guarantee a perfect family and life.

How did I develop a sense of self you might be wondering? As a child, and by nature, I was very easy-going. I tended to go with the flow and behave in a pleasing way most of the time. I think I had an innate fear of getting in trouble. Was this because of subtle messages that I could be sent back? I don't know, but perhaps.

At some point I must have decided that eventually I would be in charge of my life. All I needed to do was bide my time. So, I did. I kept my grades up, seldom got into trouble and lived as the practically-perfect child. If I have any regrets in my life, it is that I didn't raise a lot more hell as a teenager. I was way too easy!

The years went by and I explored many different interests and careers. It was only in reunion that my life started to make sense to me. Aside from the aforementioned interests of reading and crochet, I learned that my approach to life is very similar to Jackie's; we think alike, laugh alike, and have other similar interests. It was so validating to learn that I had found most of myself over the years and without the usual touchstones that most people have from being raised amongst their "people."

Through reunion, I was able to feel comfortable with who I am. It truly was a rebirth of self.

FIFTY YEARS IN 13 DAYS:
A MOTHER/DAUGHTER REUNION

Jackie Maher and Katie DeCosse (Authors)

Available on Amazon

https://www.amazon.com/Fifty-Years-13-Days-Daughter-ebook/dp/B007D620A2

CHAPTER 6

Ninety Years Young and Finding Family

By E. Irene Theis

Saturday, July 30th, 2016, was the special day when I first met Stephanie, my granddaughter, and Susan, my great-granddaughter.

When my daughter, Denise Renee Carter, passed away almost two years ago. I promised her to look out for her daughter, Laura, who is now 27 years old and grew up as an only child of Denise and Bruce. After the funeral, Laura and I spent a lot of time together. She wanted to know everything about her Mom. Also, she had known that she might have a sibling and wanted me to share everything I could remember about her mother's first pregnancy 49 years ago.

After telling Laura everything as I remembered it, I suggested that we could contact the church and the Lutheran Social Service that helped us to see what we could find out. I planned to contact them myself but gave Laura all the information I could remember

Soon, Laura told me she had contacted Lutheran Social Service, and they were sharing information with her about her half-sister, Stephanie Swenson. Then Stephanie came to Wisconsin to meet with Laura. Laura told Stephanie that they had a 90-year-old grandmother still active. Laura shared a picture and emails from Stephanie with me.

When Laura asked me what I wanted to do next, I told her that she and Stephanie should be the one to make decisions about where, when, and how we should meet. Laura suggested meeting at my apartment rather than a restaurant for privacy.

Saturday, Ben, Laura's boyfriend, and Laura arrived first at 1:30. Ben helped out by staying upstairs while Laura and I went downstairs to greet Stephanie, and Susan, Stephanie's daughter, and my new only great-granddaughter, when they arrived. Since I live in Woodland Mounds, a Security Building, we needed to meet them, let them in, and show them the way to my 3rd-floor apartment.

I had seen pictures, but it was so exciting to actually meet and hug my new granddaughter, who I had only seen once through the glass window at the hospital for about two minutes, and her daughter, Susan. Stephanie was 49, and oddly, Susan is 27, the same age as Laura.

They brought snacks, and I prepared beverages. Although I had prepared written materials to share, we sat down and shared by talking, and of course, it started mostly with me. It was painful to go back to those difficult days on Upton Avenue North in north Minneapolis, but it was important to tell things the way they were. I told her about taking Denise to the hospital before she was born, and I did break down tearfully when I told her about standing by the glass partition, looking at a newborn beautiful baby girl, who I could not touch but only look at for a few minutes. Then I was told I had to take Denise away as the adoptive parents were coming to pick up the baby and name her. I felt like I was back at that time and place 49 years ago.

Stephanie bears a great resemblance to my daughter, Denise, her biological mother. We saw pictures of her adopted family, mother, father, and brother, all of who have now passed away.

Since Denise passed away, Laura has spent a lot of time with me talking about Denise. I tried to make her feel she was not alone. We all felt that the timing of our meeting was just right for all of us. Stephanie and Susan looked at pictures of my son, Dan, and his family, sons Ryan and Aaron, Anna, who was adopted at birth, and my twin granddaughters, Mandy and Nicki, born about ten months after Anna was adopted. We explained how different that adoption was, as Dan and Stacey met the parents and grandparents at the hospital, and the biological grandparents come to Staples to visit Anna on special occasions. Stephanie lives in Underwood, Minnesota, and works in Fergus Falls, not far from Staples, where Dan lives. Dan is anxious to meet Stephanie and Susan. I told him that I want Laura to make the arrangements with Stephanie as the most important thing to me is that both Laura and Stephanie are comfortable with the timing.

Who would have thought that so many wonderful events could come about after my 90th birthday? Imagine meeting my granddaughter finally after 49 years. Imagine meeting my first and only great-grandchild.

LAURA, IRENE, STEPHANIE, SUSAN

CHAPTER 7

Stephanie and Her Friends, Who Are Family

By E. Irene Theis

My new granddaughter, Stephanie, invited me to lunch today to meet her friends.

Since her adoptive father, mother and brother all passed away, she considers these friends her family.

KIM WARD, STEPHANIE SWANSON,
GRANDMA IRENE, SHARON MARK,
LORI MOXNESS, BRENDA S.

Stephanie planned to surprise them, but did tell them I was coming just before I arrived. Stephanie met me at the door of the restaurant, and then took me back to the table to join her family/friends as she calls them. I was pleasantly surprised at the greeting I received—hugs from all.

As Stephanie and I talked, they were laughing as they noticed gestures and manners of mine that were the same as Stephanie's. They pointed out ways I moved my hands, wrist, and so on when talking and said it's just the way Stephanie does. When I apologized for talking too much, they said, "Hey, we are used to it."

Her friends are from Fergus Falls where I have spent a great deal of time over the years, both with relatives and my involvement with Minnesota Business and Professional Women. There is still an organization in Fergus Falls, but the membership is a younger group than the ones I worked with in 1992 when I was Minnesota State President.

When Stephanie informed me, she was buying my lunch, I objected, but then, as she insisted, I accepted, telling her how nice that was, because it reminded me that Denise always paid for my lunch.

Denise, the oldest of my children, did so much for me these last few years before she passed away. I am happy that both Laura, Denise's only other child, and myself have found Stephanie and that we can become her family too.

ADOPTION MATTERS!

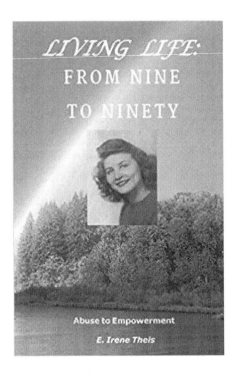

LIVING LIFE: FROM NINE TO NINETY: ABUSE TO EMPOWERMENT 2ND EDITION

By E. Irene Theis

Paperback and eBook available on Amazon.

https://www.amazon.com/Living-Life-Ninety-Abuse-Empowerment/dp/1722117796

CHAPTER 9

A Precious Gift

By Lois Miller Caswell

August 26, 1968

Written for my beautiful daughter

Carrin Marie Caswell Loken

Oh my, where do I begin? We had waited so long and longed for children it didn't seem like we would ever be Mommy and Daddy. We had been disappointed so many times, but with Grandpa Miller's encouragement, decided to visit with Lutheran Social Services and look into adoption. We were so blessed to meet and work with Marge Peterson, whom we will never forget. Grandpa had a good friend that had adopted two children, and they were so very happy. We decided we would look into it.

We first met with Ms. Peterson in February or March, and she said our wait would probably be about six months. In the meantime, Dad had some serious issues with his stomach and was in and out of the hospital several times and also out of work quite a bit so we wondered if that would cause a problem, but Marge assured us she knew we wouldn't ask for a child unless we knew we could care for him or her.

In the middle of August, I called Marge to ask her if we should go on vacation the next week or stay around and wait for our baby. She assured us we should go and told us there were seven families ahead of us, and it would be a couple of months yet, so off we went camping for a week, I am not even sure where.

Soon vacation was over and I was back at work on Monday, August 26, trying to get back in the swing of things when Dad appeared about 9:00 am. And said, "Hi Mom." It didn't register and I asked what he was doing there, and again, he said, "Hi Mom," I just came to tell you we are going to pick up our baby daughter this afternoon at 3:00. I couldn't believe my ears ...this afternoon??? I poured a cup of coffee (and I never drank coffee) and just sort of sat in a daze, I guess. Everything was kind of a blur after that. I had previously arranged that the closer to another office would take my place when our baby came, but guess what...he was on vacation that week. I had to get a closing ready and done before I could leave to pick you up. It turns out that you were born in Ramsey County and the other couples waiting for a baby all lived in Ramsey County, and since it was a closed adoption, you couldn't be placed in Ramsey County. I know that was simply God's hand in the plan because you were truly meant for us.

The good Lord had to be with me getting the papers ready, and the closing done without a mistake, I think I just went through the motions, at last, we were on our way. Thank goodness your room had been ready for weeks so all we had to do was get some food and we were good.

We got to LSS, and Marge had us wait a minute. It seemed like hours until the door opened, and in, she came with the most precious little lady dressed in a delicate light blue two-piece outfit with lace around the collar. You looked at us as if to say, "Will you be my Mommy and Daddy?" Big, big eyes, but no smile. Our hearts melted! It was love at first sight. How precious and wonderful and perfect you were. I just remember how full of love and joy we were at that moment. We were soon on our way to visit Great Grandma Caswell, who lived only a few blocks away. We hadn't told anyone else, so everyone was as surprised as we were. Great

Grandma was especially pleased that she was the very first in the family to see and hold you. After all, you were her first adopted great grandbaby and that was really special.

It was just after supper by the time we got to Grandma and Grandpa Millers. Grandpa was in his chair in the living room reading and Grandma doing dishes at the kitchen sink when we walked in the back door. Grandma looked at us as we came in, and she smiled, and her eyes welled up with tears as she got her hands out of the dishwater. Dad walked over to Grandpa and laid you in his arms, and I took his picture. I don't think he knew I did. You can't imagine the grin he had on his face when he said: "What do we have here?" They were both so very happy and thrilled.

We didn't have time to get to Grandma and Grandpa Caswell's, but everyone came to our house to meet you the next evening. They weren't quite sure what to think of it all either, but everyone was delighted to see our beautiful little daughter.

You seemed to settle in just fine except for one thing. We soon discovered that you were used to being walked to sleep. I think we did that first night because everything was so different, but that was the last time! Soon you learned that we would just let you cry yourself to sleep, and it was no more problem.

You had been in the same foster care since you left the hospital, so you were used to only one family, but I don't think they had much time to hold you because you didn't really like to be held very much. You did like to be in your infant seat always near us, and you liked to be talked to a lot. That worked really well because I had to continue to get my work done at home on the dining room table, so I was glad you were happy in the seat. I did take the following week off so we could get really settled in and used to each other. I think Dad had used his vacation time but he worked 3-11, so he was home most of the day with us. When I had to go back to work, you would go over to Sue Tomczyk's when Dad had to leave for work and stay with her until I got home. It was only a couple of hours so it worked well, and you enjoyed their four kiddos.

Dad was an awesome babysitter. He played with you all day and the house looked like it when I got home. But oh, you had so much fun. He made things for you to play with like a mobile out of fish line and teething rings. Today that would have been unsafe, but you did fine with it. You loved to talk to the other baby in the playpen. Dad put a mirror in there for you, and you loved that baby.

It was awesome when I'd get calls from Dad that said: "Carri just rolled over, or she just did this or that." I have to admit I was a little jealous, but I probably got to see some firsts also.

Remember when I said we didn't get many smiles at first. You were the best baby, never fussed, and were just happy to be near us, but not many smiles. One night I was sitting on the floor, folding diapers, and Dad was holding you in his lap when we heard a funny noise. I said, "What was that?" and we heard it again. It was your giggling! You were practicing, and you started giggling and smiling from that night on and became our "Bubblehead" always happy and smiling. I think you were six weeks old. You had only been with us for about a week. We were thrilled!

You didn't always like to eat your vegetables, but it seemed to go better if we sang Yankee Doodle, therefore your nickname of "Punkin doodle."

We have many more fun stories remembering your childhood, but no day better than the first time we held you in our arms, and you became ours forever. Our God is so good, and He had a much better plan for our family than we could ever have imagined.

We love you, Carri Marie, more than words can ever say. You have brought so much joy to our lives all these years. Thank you for being our wonderful first daughter. We celebrate you on your Adopted Birthday being so thankful God blessed us with you.

Our Love,

Mom and Dad

Untitled

A U T H O R   U N K N O W N

She's a little bit of sunshine
She's a smile to light our days
She will steal our hearts and
Keep them with her warm
            endearing ways
She's our precious little daughter
With a sweetness from above
Who will fill our years with laughter
And our lives with lots of love.

CHAPTER 8

The Most Wonderful Phone Call

By Lois Miller Caswell

Written for our son, Robert Dean Caswell

It started out to be a pretty ordinary Saturday morning, October l7, 1970, when our phone rang. It was Marge Peterson, our caseworker from Lutheran Social Services. "Good Morning," she said. "I know this is going to be a long wait for you, but I needed to give you some time to prepare for your new son whom you can pick up on Monday." She went on to explain that she knew we were ready for a small, probably younger little boy, but our son was five months old and weighed 22 pounds. No six months or year-old sizes, she said, you will want to have at least size two.

We were so excited and grateful, but my how could we wait until Monday to hold and cuddle our son? This proves once again that God always knows best and is always in control. Marge told us that your birth mother could not decide what to do so you had been placed in a foster home where you stayed until she made her decision to give you to us. Carri, who was two and a half and so ready for a brother, and you became instant playmates. She could hold you, feed you, and play with you by the hour on the floor or where ever. You became friends forever instantly.

Since we had requested a son, Grandpa Miller had chosen your name, Robert, and we added Dean for Dad since that is how he was known back then. There were already two Harold Caswell's in our family, so that would have been too complicated.

After we got off the phone, we just looked at each other hugged each other and didn't quite know where to start, but we were soon going through the things you could use from Carri and set out on a shopping trip to find at least a few things in size 2 for you to get started with. Turns out, they were even a bit small.

Would Monday ever get here? It sure didn't seem like it, but it gave us time to try to explain to Carri that we were going to have her new baby brother here soon, and to get everything ready.

I will never forget the chunky sweet wide-eyed little boy in a yellow outfit as Marge brought you in to see us for the first time. You were so sweet it was love at first sight, and when I held you for the first time, I realized 22 pounds was no little baby! We were so happy to have you in our arms, and soon, we were on our way to Great Grandma Caswell's home, which was just a few blocks away from LSS. She was always the first of our family that got to see our babies (that is until Kris arrived). We hadn't told her, so she was surprised and ever so pleased.

Finally, we were on our way home, and this time we invited Grandma and Grandpa to our house so we could get you home and settled. We told them you had arrived instead of surprising them. I guess we couldn't keep it any longer, either. I don't think they ever forgot that when they got there, they found you and I having a tug of war over you eating your vegetables. I'd put them in your mouth, and you'd spit them out. Part of that was that you had a pretty bad case of bronchitis, and part was that you just plain didn't like veggies. You did like to eat, however, and your Foster Mom fed you whenever you wanted to eat. That changed the day you came home.

Because of your cough and bronchitis, you slept for the first couple of weeks in the wind-up swing. You were such a good baby and seemed to fit right in without any problems. Carri kept you busy and entertained and you her. Our family was perfect!

Grandpa and Grandma Miller especially were so thrilled with you both. Grandma and Grandpa Caswell loved you both too, but you were two of many grandkids for them, and it was nothing new, and you were the first two for the Millers. My you would have thought they were the first grandparents in the world! They were here or had you over for any reason they could think of, just any reason to see you.

It was only about a month after you joined us that we were at church for a Thanksgiving service, and we were all to go to the altar and thank God for something we were thankful for. Grandpa was holding you, and before we knew it, he was on his way up with you. No one had to guess for a minute what he was thankful for. You and Grandpa spent many wonderful hours together doing woodwork.

It was fun to watch you grow, but you did everything different than Carri had done. So, everything was a surprise again. We were glad you were you. You rolled around instead of crawling, and I don't think you actually crawled until you were about a year old. You didn't have to cause you got around just fine that way. We didn't know if you were ever going to learn to walk, but we had gone camping in June after your first birthday and you hated to crawl in the grass, so all of a sudden you got up and walked, or should I say started to run, because you were never still after that. Carri did a lot of talking for you, but you learned to hold your own and speak for yourself before long.

Because we didn't know exactly when you were coming, I still worked for Charles Adams Real Estate, and Dad took care of you and Carri till about 2:00 when he had to go to work, and you both went across the street to Sue Tomczyks until I got home about 5:00. Dad worked 3-11 as a mechanic. Soon I was able to work from home as a Real Estate Closer and only went out for closings when we had a sitter come in for you both.

You two could get into more stuff while I was working. My office was our dining room, and I tried to make phone calls and get papers typed while you were sleeping, but most days, I ended up working at night after you had both gone to sleep. What one of you couldn't think of the other could.

I did figure a way to keep you busy while I had to get phone calls done. We fastened play phones on the kitchen cupboard so you could talk on the phone too, and you were allowed to play in the pot and pan cupboard. Most days, you took everything out, and the two of you crawled in the cupboard. At least I knew where you were.

I have lots of other stories to write about your childhood days, but we thank the Lord each day for knowing what was best for us by bringing you to us. We are so proud of you Bob. You have brought us so much love and joy and some grey hair too. You and I have spit lots of "veggies" at each other as you were growing up, and as you grew so tall, I'd have to back you in a corner and get your attention that way. Thank you for being our special son. For being true to yourself and developing your own personality. We are so proud of the wonderful man, husband, and Christian father you have become. Now we are the proud doting grandparents of Clayton and Claire. God is so good. We love you, Bob. Thank you for being our wonderful son.

Mom and Dad

October 16, 2015

P.S. I thought that was the longest "labor" I had ever heard of until poor Lisa had to wait almost a week for Clayton to be born.

.

A Boy Is

AUTHOR UNKNOWN

Trust with dirt on its face,
Beauty with a cut on its finger.
Wisdom with bubble gum in its
hair, and the
Hope of the future with
A frog in its pocket.

CHAPTER 10

Meeting Shin Hyun Ok

A STORY FOR DAMON, HER YOUNG
SON, AGE FOUR

By Esther Holgate

There once was a very little girl who was born in the far-away country of South Korea. She was a dear, healthy baby, but she had a big problem. Sadly, her mother and father were not able to take care of her. They wanted to be sure their lovely daughter, Hyun, would have good care and a home. They learned about an orphanage, Il San, in the big city of Seoul, where babies could be given to foster families for care while waiting to be adopted by forever families. Hyun would have to wait, but the people at Il San would provide a good home until they found a special family for her. So, the mother and father brought their little girl to the Il San Orphanage.

In Minnesota, thousands of miles away, there was an American family—a dad, a mom, and two little boys. They lived in a nice house in a small, friendly town. The dad and mom were happy with their two sons, but they wanted a daughter to complete their family. It would be a fine idea to find a baby girl who needed a home, they thought.

In Minneapolis, there was a group of people who were finding families for homeless Korean children. They would help find a little girl, but many other families were waiting, too. The dad and mom and two brothers waited their turn for a year-and-a-half.

Then one day, a telephone call came. Yes. Shin Hyun Ok, age twenty-one months, could come by plane with a group of Korean children and caretakers. They would arrive in Chicago on September 10th. However, she had an ear infection. Did the family still want her? Did they <u>want</u> her? What a silly question. Of course, they wanted her.

How excited the American family was! On the

calendar, the boys counted out the days when their baby would arrive. The family needed to buy her a bed, and a chest of drawers for her new clothes, and some girl-toys from Target. The mom bought a round-trip plane ticket to Chicago to get her, while the boys and their dad would come later to the Minneapolis airport to bring them home by car. Early in the morning on Sept. 10th, the dad and the boys took the mom to the airport. "Hurry home with our baby," they said.

Soon the mom was in Chicago's very large airport. She went to a special room where the other parents were waiting. The plane was delayed. Still more hours to wait! They would need to stay overnight in a motel, too. The mom called home to tell about the delay and to make a reservation at a motel.

Finally, the plane from Korea arrived late that night. The waiting families gathered excitedly to meet the plane. Out of the plane came eleven little children, one-by-one, some being carried by caretakers, some walking. The name of each child was announced. Then came a call: "Shin Hyun, OK." "That's our girl," exclaimed the mom as she rushed forward and reached out her arms to her new daughter.

But Hyun was crying. She was afraid to leave her Korean helper for this strange person whom she didn't know. The mom looked different and used words she didn't know. No one could explain to her what was happening because she was too little to understand. She was hungry and tired. The mom held her tenderly and bought her a cup of milk and a hotdog. Hyun drank the milk and ate the bun, but the wiener looked odd. She had never seen one before and decided not to touch it.

Hyun, dressed in very warm clothes, was hot and uncomfortable, but she could walk well in her Korean rubber shoes. She held the mom's hand, coming with her through the airport to a waiting car, which took them to a motel.

Once in the motel room, she was afraid she would be lost or have to go to another stranger, so she held onto the new mom tightly and would not let go. Hugging each other, they got ready for the night and crawled onto the big bed. Hyun slept, but sometimes she had to give out a big sob to help her get through the night. In the morning, she opened her eyes to see the same mom beside her. The mom smiled, but Hyun would not smile back. The mom was worried. She looked deep into Hyun's sad, dark eyes and wondered what would help her little girl smile.

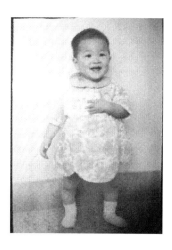

Into the big plane, they went, leaving Chicago behind. High in the air, on their way back to Minnesota, a stewardess came by to say hello and attach an airline emblem, a "winged" pin onto Hyun's dress. She soon returned with juice and a sweet roll nicely frosted over the top. The little girl took the roll, tasted the frosting, turned to the mom, and finally gave her the biggest smile. That smile warmed the mom's heart and made her happy. Hyun would be happy, too, and she would be all right.

An hour later, the plane landed at the Minneapolis airport. Slowly the people came off the plane. The dad and his two boys stood nearby, eagerly looking. "Where was Mom? Where was the new sister? Ah, there they are!" There were big hugs and excited talking. Hyun did not cry this time; she was ready for their hugs and smiles. This was her family, and she belonged to them forever.

Sometime later, I wrote a poem about meeting Angela and bringing her home.

MEETING HYUN

Little Asian child

Come so far---alone,

It was a silver bird that brought you

To a land of abrupt change.

Little padding feet shod in rubber shoes,

You follow me wordlessly through the airport.

An occasional great sob heaves from your tiny breast.

Shin Hyun Ok does not smile.

Your eyes are dark pools of mystery.

You cannot tell me.

I cannot tell you.

Clinging will have to suffice, for now.

So we spend a motel night together, coping.

Morning comes after the long hours.

We eat our somber breakfast

And board the plane for home.

Danish rolls and juice are served mid-air.

Hyun takes a bite into the frosted treat,

Looks at me, and smiles.

Our daughter warms my heart

By Esther Holgate

CHAPTER 11

.

My Adoption Story

By Ann Kalin

My name is Ann Kalin, and I am the mother of two adopted children.

As the oldest daughter in a family of eight children, I was often asked to help my mom with the younger children. My love for children and desire to be a mother started then. I enjoyed taking care of the little ones as they were like my dolls, and I would dress them and play with them. I was also praised by both my parents for being the responsible big sister. This made me feel important and loved. However, like many young women of the '60s and '70s, I was "liberated," so I went to college and postponed my motherhood for a career. On my thirtieth birthday, I decided I was ready to start the motherhood chapter of my life. My husband, Jerry, was also ready to start being a father. We are both planners, and we thought we had a great "plan."

Jerry and I were two healthy adults and assumed that becoming pregnant and having children would occur naturally and quickly. It didn't. Unfortunately, after many disappointments, our "plan" was not working. At that time, we were living in Washington, D.C., so we found and saw a pioneer in infertility, Dr. Georgeanna Jones, at Johns Hopkins University Hospital in Baltimore, Maryland. After many tests on both Jerry and me, it was confirmed there were no physical problems preventing us from conceiving a child, so we took the step with fertility drugs, DNC, and other procedures. Since those were unsuccessful, we were counseled to try in-vitro fertilization (IVF), which at that time, 1978, was in its infancy. It would have been the next step.

Jerry, who was born and raised in Minnesota, had wanted to return there someday. When a great job opportunity came along, one too good to pass up, we jumped on it and moved to Eden Prairie. Wanting to continue our fertilization process, we asked Dr. Jones to recommend a fertility expert in Minneapolis. She did, but unfortunately, it soon became clear that the fertility clinics in the Twin Cities, and especially IVF, were not as advanced as those at Johns Hopkins.

Meanwhile, the time clock was ticking, and both Jerry and I were frustrated with the tests and procedures, which were often repeats of what was done at John Hopkins. We immediately applied for adoption at Children's Home Society shortly after moving to Minnesota. It was about two years later when the priest announced that Catholic Charities were accepting seventy applicants for adoption, we became excited and applied the following day; we were the sixty-ninth applicant accepted. Timing is everything! We were told that it would take two-three years to receive a child; we were resigned to wait. We now had our names in two adoption agencies.

Jerry and I continued our careers and were building a new home. Within one-year, Catholic Charities called us for the "home study," which involved visiting our home, and asking questions about us and our potential parenting abilities. Questions included: how would we discipline our child? Do we live in a safe neighborhood? How would I balance my career and our child? I guess we had the right answers as things started moving quickly, and we were tenth on the list of possible adoption candidates.

About six months later, I received an unexpected call at work; it was Catholic

Charities. They said, "We have a baby boy who would love to have you and Jerry as parents. Would you like to pick him up tomorrow?" Tomorrow! What an emotional explosion. In less than 24 hours, we would be picking up our son, Eric!

Oddly, just two days before this phone call, my mother had called and shared a dream with me that she had. In the dream, it was clear that we adopted a baby boy. Note, we had not requested a certain gender. My mom had always had a sixth sense when it came to her eight children. I had taken this information to heart and purchased a crib that was still in its box in the garage.

We were moving into our new house, with a baby boy within the week, and I had nothing for the baby except a crib, per my mom's dream. Most women have nine months to prepare for this day, but not me. I immediately went shopping with a mother friend to get the necessary baby items.

I started writing a journal for each of my children so that I could capture the special moments and emotions I felt at the time. The following is an entry in Eric's journal on the day of his adoption, March 11, 1980. He was only 25 days old.

The drive to the adoption agency seemed miles away, and I insisted your dad drive faster. Once we arrived, we talked to many people, but I just wanted to see you. Finally, they brought you into the room wearing the special outfit that we had picked out for you. You had big rosy cheeks, white skin, and dark hair... you were beautiful! Your biological mom made a special blanket for you and wrote a letter to you explaining why she could not keep you. We agreed to share this letter with you at 21 years old. We did not read this letter for a long time as our emotions were soaring.

A few weeks later, after reading her letter, we learned that she had named him Matthew, which means, "Gift from God." I am so glad we were in church the day they announced Catholic Charities were accepting applicants for adoption. Our Eric has truly been a gift from God. We have enjoyed a lifetime (now 39 years) with our son.

Eric spent the first week with us sleeping in a dresser drawer in our bedroom in our old house before moving into his nursery in our new home. I am sure the adoption agency would NOT approve. At that time, we had a dog named Raggedy, who loved to fetch a racquetball. At four months old, Eric would toss the ball to Raggedy, and she would bring the ball back to him full of saliva and dirt. This game of catch went on for hours. Balls were Eric's favorite toy, and he went on to play soccer, baseball, and football in grade school and high school. He is a great athlete.

Eric graduated from the University of Minnesota with a degree in journalism and currently runs a small business, Olympic Pools. He has grown into a tall, handsome young man with a beautiful daughter named Valentina, who looks like a female version of Eric. I am blessed to be her Nana.

There are so many memories and milestones in these 39 years. However, one especially stands out; the day Eric met his biological mom. It started with a registered letter from his biological mom when Eric was 18-years-old. Because it was a private adoption, by law, no communications between the biological mother and adopted child could occur before age 21. In her letter, she asked for confirmation that Eric was her biological son. She had sent baby photos when he was first born, and there was no doubt that Eric was indeed her biological son. Her name is Ann. Because Eric's name and pictures were in the local newspapers for his football accomplishments, Ann figured out who he was. Eric looks exactly like his biological mom. In the letter, she requested to meet Eric. Although Jerry and I have always been open with both our children's adoption, Jerry and I struggled with the decision whether or not to share this letter with Eric. He was only a senior in high school at the time. We finally shared that letter with him the summer before he went to college, and he quickly answered, "I am not ready for this."

After two years in college, Eric decided he wanted to meet his biological mother. I remember asking him how he wanted to do it. He simply said, "Let's have her family over for lunch." It was so simple for him but difficult for me. The following is an entry I wrote in Eric's journal.

Lunch at our house sounded like a great idea until that day they arrived. I felt total panic! All of that disappeared when they arrived, and I opened our front door to a warm and friendly woman in a lavender dress, holding a bouquet of flowers from her garden. Following her was her husband, Eric (go figure), and her three biological children. We basically talked non-stop from noon until 4:30. We shared tears and laughter, and I must admit she felt like a sister. Maybe that is because she has four sisters as I do and knows what it's like to share love. I asked her why she chose us for Eric's parents. We were number ten on the waiting list and expected to wait another year. She said she decided to, "Let God choose for me," and our names came to her. God knew we would love Eric and pulled some strings for us that day.

Although intellectually, I accepted Eric's biological mom coming into his life, I still felt afraid of losing him. He just left for college, and that was difficult enough letting go. But I realized after sharing so many stories with Ann about Eric and our family that we had 19-plus years of Eric as our son, which his biological mom would never experience. She would never experience Eric's first day of school, the excitement on Christmas day playing Nintendo (all day), big wheel kamikaze, skiing vacations spent as a family especially when we drove the RV to Snowmass, or the special moments of love a mother and son share while growing up. Those are "our" memories of Eric. Her kids were young at the time, so that she will have her own experiences and memories with her two biological sons. She will have a different relationship with Eric than with her sons that grow up with her. Since that initial meeting, Eric has spent time getting to know his half brothers and sisters as well as Ann. I no longer feel that I will lose our son. There is lots of room for love in life, and I know Eric's relationship with Ann and her family has become something special.

Now for Chapter Two of My Adoption Story... Heather, "The Charmer."

Jerry and I had applied to Children's Home Society (CHS) as soon as we moved to Minnesota and two years before we had applied to Catholic Charities. CHS allowed two infants to be adopted by one family, but Catholic Charities would only allow one adopted infant per family. Timing is everything, as we would have only one adopted child if Catholic Charities was our second adoption option. Because we specifically requested an infant girl, and there was a longer waiting list for girls, we expected to wait one or two more years for our next child. As it was, we had already waited four years. It was the weekend of July 4, 1981, and the fireworks were about to begin!

Jerry's sister's family was visiting from California, and everyone went tubing down the Apple River in remote Wisconsin while I stayed home with Eric, who was only 15 months old. Eric was asleep in my arms when the phone rang, and I scrambled to answer it with one hand. After my stumbling, "Hello," I heard, "Hello, this is Steve Blons from CHS, and we have a baby girl for you and Jerry."

My response was an abrupt, "Let me call you back." Most adopting parents would be jumping for joy, but I was terrified of having two babies so close together in age. I knew from my mom's experience with her eight children (all about two years apart) this would be difficult. All I wanted was to talk to Jerry and decide what WE should do.

Remember, this is 1981, and there were no cell phones for immediate, easy communication. As the hours crept by, I was concerned that CHS would close for the day and that the little girl might not be available tomorrow, but all I could do was wait until Jerry returned home. During that time, my planning brain was in full gear, and I convinced myself that the timing was not good. It was the longest afternoon of my life. When Jerry finally called from his parent's home late that evening, I explained what happened. Without any hesitation or doubt, his immediate response was, "I guess we will have our little girl tomorrow." We talked, and Jerry pointed out how we have planned everything in our lives, but sometimes things just happen for the best. Life is not always a neatly packaged plan. I do love Jerry for his quick decision and clear thinking. Without it, there would never be Heather in our lives.

Because it was late, CHS was closed, and I feared we lost our chance at adopting this little girl. The next morning, we called Steve Blons and asked if this little girl was still available, and he confirmed that she was waiting for us. We had already picked names for both children long before any adoptions. Her name would be

Heather. Once again, we had less than 24 hours to pull everything together. We had a bassinet (no dresser drawer for this princess) and many essential baby items, however, I went shopping and bought the cutest "coming home" outfit; sunshine yellow rose buds with lots of lace, along with a matching bonnet and shoes. This is the entry from my journal to Heather:

We went to CHS about 11:30 on July 6, 1981. Eric stayed home With Mrs. Clough, who babysat Eric when I worked three days a week. There was a cute nursery with a couch and rocking chair, and we waited until your foster mom brought you into the room and gave you to me. You hugged me and formed to my body like a glove. At that moment, all my doubts flushed from my head. You were so lovable and beautiful. You looked like a baby doll as your face and body were so petite... so feminine. The foster mom had written notes and said that you were a good baby and only cried when something was wrong. We would later learn that she was so right. At five weeks, you were sleeping through the night. I could not believe what a blessing that was with two young children. When we got home, Mrs. Clough and Eric were waiting. When she held you, she immediately nicknamed you, "The Charmer." How could she know how perfect that name would be for you?

Just a few observations I wrote in your journal

during the first few days we had you:

You love to be held, and you were often strapped in a baby pouch on my chest You love your pacifier, and you suck really loud when you have your bottle. You sleep with your butt in the air. Did I mention you were sleeping through the night? You pass gas loudly...*we nicknamed you, "Little Toot."*

All of the above observations we found were true of our Heather. I took six months off from work to totally experience being a mother of two young children. Life was good. We lived in a young neighborhood with lots of children. Heather formed a lifetime friendship with one girl, Angie Cramer. We had the perfect basement for kids to play in. We painted a haunted house on the cinderblock wall for Halloween one year and they added to it over the years. We painted a big wheel race track on the basement floor so they could ride their big wheels in the winter. There was a hideaway room under the stairs which had a door and a quiet place to read with bean bag chairs. This had a favorite place for Heather, and she and Angie played school here often. We continued to use Mrs. Clough for occasional daycare, and again when I returned to work, she loved the kids dearly! It was Mrs. Clough's first experience caring for a baby girl as she raised four boys. Because of this and Heather's personality, Mrs. Clough nicknamed

Heather, the "Charmer." It fit her perfectly...better than "Little Toot"!

My sister Judy had a baby girl, Carleigh, in November 1981, only three months after we adopted Heather. I had visions of Heather and Carleigh being best friends and cousins. Judy lived in the state of Virginia, so we did not see each other often, but when we did, our daughters were our focus. Judy also had two sons; one is Eric's age, and the boys had fun by themselves. The situation changed when Carleigh was diagnosed with a fatal genetic disorder at the age of 5 years old. It started with her forgetting what she had already learned, such as colors, numbers, and letters. This genetic disorder was destroying her brain. Her mental state deteriorated quickly, and her physical state deteriorated gradually. By age 12, Carleigh was in a wheelchair, was fed through a tube in her stomach as she could not swallow. Judy and her husband could no longer care for her at home and had to put her in a facility for handicapped children. Doctors did not expect Carleigh to live past 16 years old. Carleigh died at the age of 21. During those years, my sister's pain was my pain. We cried together a lot during our phone calls and visits. Heather became a more precious gift. Many times, during Heather's teenage years, when I wanted to ship her out of the house, I thought of Carleigh and was thankful to have a teenager to argue with.

Judy and Carleigh taught me true, unconditional love. They were a blessing in my life through those teenage years with Heather.

I have been blessed to continue with all the events in my daughter's life. Heather went to Mankato State University, earning a degree in Nursing. She first worked at Abbott Hospital in Minneapolis, rooming with her friend Angie until she met Dan, who is now her husband. Much to my surprise, Heather married him within eight months of meeting him. They both like to ski so they moved to Park City, Utah, shortly after they were married, where Heather worked as an RN at the Orthopedic Hospital in Park City, Utah, for a year. She became pregnant and returned to Minnesota. On May 5, 2012, our first grandchild, Vivian, was born. Seeing Vivian for the first time, all I could see was Heather. It was love at first sight for me. Her name fits her to a tee. "La Vie." She is full of life!

Heather, Dan, and Vivian moved to Eau Claire, Wisconsin, a few years after returning from Utah, and it was a sad day for Nana and Papa! There have been many road trips and visits since then. They tried for four years to have a second child and because they were unable to conceive, they applied for adoption. When adoption didn't work out, they decided to have IVF procedures done. Heather has a good understanding of the emotions of infertility having experienced the failed procedures, medications and disappointments of not conceiving wanting another child so badly. Finally, after one failed attempt and many shots of hormones required for IVF, they decided to plant two embryos, and both successfully started growing. The twins were born. On December 15 and December 16, 2018, and Vivian became a big sister to Matilda (Tilly) and Theodore (Teddy), respectively. Teddy was born two hours after Tilly, hence the different birthdays. Vivian was six-years-old. All three children bring much joy to our lives, but it is overwhelming taking care of THREE children so young.

Since this is about adoption, I would like to mention how Heather met her biological mom. There were two significant events. When she was 13-years-old, CHS sent us a letter from her biological grandmother, who was dying from lung cancer. She was seeking information about Heather. Heather, Jerry, and I agreed to provide information, so I wrote back to her, as did Heather. Heather wrote a beautiful, thoughtful letter for being only 13 years old. After these letters, we did not continue corresponding, as it was a private adoption.

The second event happened when Heather developed a fibrous cyst on her breast. As a nurse, Heather feared cancer, but a biopsy proved it to be benign. This event piqued

Heather's curiosity about her biological health background. At age 23, she reached out to CHS for more information. They connected her anonymously with her biological mother through letters written to CHS and delivered to Heather. Names and identifying information were blocked out. Heather shared those letters with me, and I was honored as some of the written communications were very personal. Her biological mother, Pauline, was only 17 when she got pregnant. She felt adoption was best for Heather. When I asked Heather if she wanted to meet Pauline, she said, "I would like to meet her through glass where I could see her, but she could not see me." They did not meet then but continued for several years to communicate with letters through CHS.

Approximately three months after Heather met Dan, it was decided that she and Dan would meet Pauline without me. It was probably the most hurtful event in all my years of motherhood. I thought that this was something a mother and daughter should share. We had shared 23 years together, whereas she had known Dan for only a few months. It was a few months after their initial meeting that I joined Heather and Pauline for lunch at a restaurant in South Minneapolis. Pauline, like Eric's biological mother, could be one of my sisters. We talked easily and enjoyed sharing family stories. Pauline has two girls; hence Heather now has two half-sisters. They are 6 and 8 years older than Heather. Within a few months, Heather and Dan set their wedding date, and much to my surprise, Heather wanted to invite Pauline to the wedding. My immediate response was, "No," and Heather couldn't understand what the big deal was. After Heather spends 23 years with her daughter, Vivian, she will understand that there can be ONLY one mother of the bride. Although Pauline didn't come to the wedding, she attended the family picnic at our home the day after the wedding.

I want to mention a final note on the biological fathers. Eric's biological father refused any responsibility or communications with his biological mom; hence, Eric never pursued meeting his biological father. Heather's biological father, Dan (interesting the thread of names in our story), has remained friends with Pauline over the years; hence Heather often sees them together for dinner or other social events. Dan is a successful lawyer in the Twin Cities but never married.

As I re-read my story, I reflect on a card that I received from a friend congratulating us on adopting Eric.

Give your children roots and wings

It was so simple when they were babies but so

profound today. I am 70 years old, and having experienced adoption and all the events that have transpired over the years, we have strived to give them family roots, both ours and their biological families. We have also allowed them to spread their wings and fly into adulthood and become who they are...two beautiful people that we love so dearly.

CHAPTER 12

She Had Me at Umma

By Carolyn Wilhelm

She had me at Umma. When she was handed to me, the person pointed at me and said, "Umma." Our newly adopted daughter instantly understood, called me Umma, and didn't let go of me for months. Literally. She was unable to be apart from me day or night.

It was not for dozens of years we learned that prior to arriving to our house in Minnesota, our little baby had lived in ten other placements in South Korea. Of course, she did not want to be separated from me for a single minute.

BETSY MEETS UMMA

February 26, 1981, Betsy Lee Wilhelm arrived on Northwest Airlines (now Delta) flight #70. At that time, Children's Home Society (our adoption agency) had flight aids who flew to South Korea and returned by air with several children. That was how it was done. Carrying her off the plane, she called, "Wilhelm baby! Wilhelm baby!" and we had our first in-person view of our new daughter. It was love at first sight.

KATH SHUN, FLIGHT AID FOR
ADOPTEES

Betsy arrived with a pre-flight report. This included her sleeping habits, which included kicking her quilt deeply – something she still does. Her vocabulary included Umma for mother, Papa for father, and bye-bye. She could already stand and walk three steps. The report said she is, "Fear with new one terribly." Now we can look back and say this was probably due to moving to different homes so often. She drank milk, standing and holding the bottle by herself. Please get out of her way. She had things to do and places to go – all within a very few feet of me.

CHILD'S PRE-FLIGHT REPORT

Child's Name: Lee, Youn Hee (F)   Case Number:800-558

Birth Date: April 17, 1980   Date of Departure:Feb. 26, 1981

Adoptive Family: M/M Cary and Carolyn Wilhelm   Airport:

Name of Escort: Destination:

Physical condition of child:

Feeding/Eating: She is fed with 200cc of milk every 3-4 hour holding a bottle by herself. She has 1 spoon of rice mixing with egg every meal time. She doesn't eat sour food and spits out something to eat if she doesn't like it.

Sleeping Habits: She sleeps from 12:30am to 9:00 and wakes at 3:00 during the night for milk. She takes a nap about 1-2:00pm for two hour. She sleeps deeply kicking her quilt.

Toilet Training: She does bowel movement once a day in good condition.

Speech: She speaks the words "Umma(mother), Papa(father), bye-bye"

Weight: 8.2kg

(Feb. 19, 1981)

Height: 690m

Ability: She stands up by herself and walks three steps. She crawls up on the desk. She shakes her body watching T.V., and does action "Doridori(turning her head) Jjakjakung(clapping), bye-bye, Anyoung(Good-bye)".

Character: She plays with new thing, and likes to draw out everything in the drawer. She cries sorrowfully if she is scolded, and she is fond of carrying on mother's back. She is fear with new one terribly and her temper is gentle.

Teething: She has two lower teeth.

Legal Status: Orphan

Legal Guardian: Kim Duk Whang(President of Eastern Child Welfare Society, Inc.)

Remarks: She prefers lukewarm milk to hot milk.

ADOPTIVE PRE-FLIGHT REPORT

Not all children arrive with helpful instructions.

The first time we saw Betsy's photo was June 6, 1980. She was, of course, living in Korea, and the next picture includes one of her foster caregivers. Once we saw the photo and couldn't wait to meet our new daughter. Her name at that time was Youn Hee Lee. We kept Lee as her middle name. She was supposed to be ours when she was four months old. However, there was a coup in Korea, and all adoptions were stopped. Waiting for updates about when the adoptions might begin again was difficult. We learned at one "while you are waiting" meeting at Children's Home Society that Betsy was in a tiny minority as she was not born in a hospital as most of the Korean orphans were.

FOSTER CAREGIVER WITH BETSY

Dreaming of having a baby, I imagined I would hold the bottle for my child. I would cuddle her and watch her drink milk. Nope, she had other ideas. I tried feeding her baby food, but she preferred chili and chopped salad with Italian dressing, by the handful, thank you very much. OK, then! Once when newly arrived and we were at my Bible study group, she wanted my coffee cup. She made a fuss. They said to let her have a sip, and it would stop the behavior. We all watched in horror as she drank the whole cup in nothing flat. I made sure that it was her last coffee for many years!

In May of 1982, Betsy made the news! Well, she was in Picture Magazine for the Star Tribune Sunday section. Why? She became a United States Citizen. Our family is on the right of this picture, and she is holding an American flag. What you can't see is the tears on her face. Although rather serious, she probably didn't understand what was going on. Parents take the oath and pledge allegiance to the flag for young children at these ceremonies.

Little hands waved little flags as scores of children in the Twin Cities joined the ranks of U.S. citizens. The swearing-in ceremony took place in the courtroom of U.S. District Justice Miles Lord. The judge performed two such ceremonies that day, giving the United States 194 new citizens.

Kids become 'part of country'

Staff Photos by John Croft

By Mary Jane Smetanka
Staff Writer

For Melissa Ann Lang, becoming an American citizen meant waving the stars and stripes in a big room crowded with people and going out to an ice-cream parlor afterward.

It meant something more to Nancy and Roger Lang of Blaine, the parents of the adopted 18-month old Korean girl.

"I don't know if she really understood it, but it was real important to us," said Nancy Lang. "It meant that she's a part of this country."

Melissa was one of 16 children and 54 adults naturalized recently in Minneapolis. Last year more than 1,800 people became American citizens in monthly naturalization ceremonies in Minneapolis and St.

Fifty-four adults crowded into the federal courtroom in Minneapolis to repeat the oath of allegiance.

At the welcome home party, which was immediately after the ride to our house from the airport, about 30 people met Betsy. At that time, we announced a closely held secret we had known for only two weeks. Carolyn's doctor had figured out why somethings had recently changed about her health, and Betsy was going to have a sibling in about six months.

I will say it was much easier to simply drive to the airport and pick up a baby than go through a difficult labor and delivery!

Not only did she get a brother, but we all also moved to the Netherlands for a year when Betsy was three. Here we are by Dutch tulips. Betsy had lived on three continents by the time she was three and a half.

The name on her welcome cake was misspelled, and it read, "Welcome, **Besty** Lee." She has been the best!

CHAPTER 13

Melanie's Story

By Irene Reuteler

I know I have written this story already but wanted to put it in a word document to be saved for Melanie later in life. It was a profound experience for me and the true measure of God's love.

It began with a little girl named Heidi. She was always taking care of children. When she was three, her little brother Erik was born. She moved right in and began taking care of him. She loved him to pieces and thought he was a gift just for her. She had a natural ability to know what was needed and a willingness to provide it in whatever way she could. I actually had to hold her back as she was very happy to help out all the time. When she was in elementary school, she took care of neighbor children, even being paid to watch children during summer days.

When she and Neal wanted to start a family, they struggled with doctoring, praying, and disappointment. How could this happen? She would be a fantastic mother. What was the message? How some people that don't want or can't take care of children have them while those capable and willing can't seem to make it happen. Hard to understand.

I hurt for her and identified as much as possible since we had experienced infertility also; as had my parents. But both Mom and I were able to get pregnant ultimately. I thought for a long time that this would happen for them, but it didn't. Time, treatments, and doctoring but no results. It was watching their hopes rise every month and crash, then rise again and crash. Over and over.

One day as I was sitting in church waiting for services to start, I glanced around and noticed people sitting with their families working at controlling kids, straightening hair, and dresses. Quite unexpectedly and unbidden, a complete thought entered my mind. I knew, with a certainty that I could not explain, that Heidi and Neal would have a little girl. I didn't know when or how. I just knew it would be. It was a strong and certain knowledge. I heard no voice, just suddenly knew...It gave me comfort. But what would I do with this knowledge? I didn't know. Telling Heidi felt scary, and I would feel vulnerable. How would she hear this message? But I knew what I knew. I guarded this assurance, and it gave me comfort. It may have been months before I decided to tell Heidi. There came a time when it seemed right; I cannot say how she received it. That would be her story. I know she wanted to believe it in the worst way. I knew she believed in God's love. I hoped it would give her comfort. Time went by; more tests, shots, waiting, ups, and downs. Results negative.

At a point in time, they decided that they didn't necessarily want **their** child, they wanted **a** child. This opened the door to working with Children's Home Society. They put together their book of pictures, stories, life experiences. It wasn't long before a call came that someone wanted to meet them. That was a very exciting call. They went to meet with the prospective mother. She had given up one child several years ago and didn't want to raise this one. We learned it was a boy. Heidi hoped that part was negotiable. I, however, knew it was not. I hurt because I felt something would happen to break her heart. I knew it was to be a girl for them. Conversations between this mother and Heidi occurred regularly and then suddenly stopped.

No one heard from the mother, not Heidi, not Children's Home Society. Silence. Then Children's heard that the birth father's parents took the baby home to raise. Understandable but very hard for us to hear. Heidi was devastated beyond words. We were broken-hearted.

A few weeks later, another mother wanted to meet them. Heidi called me quite anxious. *"How can I do this again. How can I not? What do I do?"* My only advice could be to meet and see. We were nervous when they met with 16-year-old Sally and her dad. Sally didn't know what she was having or when. Her father had encouraged her to put her baby up for adoption so she could continue being a teen. The meeting was good. Heidi and Neal thought Sally was intelligent and seemed focused on following through. Another meeting was set - but it didn't happen.

Thanksgiving morning, early, November 23, 1995, Heidi and Neal got a call that Sally was in labor. Could they come for the birth? As they were entertaining both families over Thanksgiving, she called and asked if I would host it. They brought over the turkey while we got ready for the gathering. As luck would have it, the diaper bag that Heidi wanted had arrived at our house the day before. It was to be a surprise. We got the turkey; she got the diaper bag. Tears all around.

As both families gathered, we began getting

calls about the progress of Sally's labor. How provident that we were all in one place. As the afternoon wore on, it came time for me to pick up my dad, and I knew the baby would come while I was gone. No cell phones, so it was just go and hurry back. As I was returning, I saw our daughter-in-law outside, jumping up and down and laughing. I knew the baby was here. When I jumped out of the car, I said: "It's a girl." She said yes. We hugged, cried, and laughed. This was to definitely be their daughter.

Their adoption was successful, and Melanie has had contact with many of her birth parents and grandparents and extended family because everyone respected appropriate boundaries and put Melanie's feelings first. Because it was a pretty successful open adoption, Heidi, Neal, and Melanie participated in several workshops at Children's Home Society during the first few years.

Melanie now has a daughter with several involved grandmothers and great grandmothers. It has worked smoothly for 24 years and counting.

CHAPTER 14

Coping with Identity Problems

By *David Zander*

I was adopted. For the first six years of my life, I thought Rita and Jim Smith were my parents. I went to school as David Smith. I was born in London. In July 1940, During WW2, America had not yet entered the war. That did not happen until the Japanese bombed Pearl Harbor. But in Europe, England was at war with Germany. My first memories are of war, *being* carried down into an Air raid shelter during the nightly air raids. Bombs were falling. I pointed up at the sky, and Jim said that was dog fights in the sky. I wondered why dogs were fighting in the sky. A few years later, the Germans launched unpiloted V2 Rockets at England during the day. Hitler sent me a birthday present of a V2 rocket for my fourth birthday. He missed my house by about twelve miles, but the shock from the explosion blew all the windows out. Then Germany surrendered. It was peacetime, short supply of food, and a slow ending of rationing books,

I went to infant school. I was David Smith. All was quiet and peaceful until another bomb fell, this time a direct hit. Rita Smith, who I had thought was my biological mother, called me up on her lap one day and told me, "I am not your mother." Not their child; I was not the Smith family. My world shattered. I asked Rita, "Who is my mother?" Rita said, "Auntie May." Auntie May was this shadowy distant figure who came to our house about once a month. She never hugged me nor showed any sign she was my mother. It was weird. I think if Rita had hugged me and said, "But I still love you," things might not have got so emotionally messed up. But she was pregnant with her own child, and her affection for me turned off like a picket. I got down off her lap, crossed the cold kitchen, opened the big wooden door out into the garden, went around the old laundry room into the sunlight, and sat on the grass. I was surrounded by buttercups and dandelions. To this day, I hate dandelions. A tear trickled down my nose. I felt emotionally numb.

Rita and Jim Smith had been childless, but now Rita was pregnant with Susan and later Jimmy. Rita's affection for me turned off like a water tap.

I have fond memories of her husband, Jim. Jim Smith had taught me to ride a bike, kick a football. But my memories of Rita were that she transformed into the ugly stepmother, cruel, cold. It had been a clumsy adoption, more like temporary foster care. No agencies involved. I was born illegitimate. My mother had an alcoholic husband and had an affair. I must have been quite a surprise to her as she was forty when she got pregnant with me. My mother gave Rita some money every month to raise me. But why this deception of letting me think I was a Smith, that I never fully understood.

My birth certificate says, David Zander. My mother was May Zander, married to Harry Zander. Harry had come to England from Sweden with his parents. His mother became prosperous as a dressmaker. My mother's maiden name was May West. So, I am the son of May West. I like that. It makes me laugh. The next ten years of my life were chaotic. I went back and forth between the two families. A friend who is adopted tells me that it is not correct to say May is my real mother. Does that mean there is a false mother? The correct term for May Zander is she is my biological mother. She was likable, kind. But unfortunately, I had bonded with Rita. That stayed as a subconscious force in my mind. Who did I invite to my college graduation? Rita. Who did I want at my wedding? Rita. My mother had married Harry Zander, but he was not my biological father. I never knew my biological father or even his name. When I asked my mother, she said it was none of my business. But every kid wonders about how they are like their parent. As a teenager, I would look at a person on the other side of the street and think is that my father. I made up a story that perhaps he had been killed in the war. How can you like a father who never attempted to see you?

May and Harry slowly got their marriage back together. We called Harry "Pop." When they moved into Pop's mother's house, there was room for me. I met an older half-brother there, John Zander. I had to change schools; I went to school now as David Zander. Luckily, I passed the impotent eleven plus exam that allowed me to go to a grammar school. I was good in school.

I want to ask my readers to think about this question: what myth, fairytale, or folktale are you living? Mythologists and storytellers like Joseph Campbell say we are living these archetypal stories. Hero heroine tales, quest like Odysseus. I found one which seems to fit me; a story about two women arguing as to who is the mother. People tell me it's in the Bible, King Solomon, but I prefer the Chinese version, The Good Woman of Szechuan. Two mothers claim possession of a child. A judge puts big rope, which will tear the child apart unless one of the mothers lets go. The child is in the middle of a tug of war. The biological mother lets go. The story not perfect for me – I was pulling the rope on one side again, one mother. But that image of being trapped in the middle of a tug of war was how I saw myself – David Smith or David Zander. I even horrified a girlfriend later when I argued against monogamy – I said I think I can love two women at the same time. That's what I had been expected to do.

I want to close by telling tell you the story of Christmas with the Zander family. It was so different from the Smiths. The Smiths were traditional English with Father Christmas bringing presents down the chimney at dawn, whereas in the Zander tradition, presents were under the Christmas tree, and on Christmas Day, the youngest child distributed presents from under the Christmas tree after Christmas dinner. The decorations were different. The Smiths decorated a Christmas tree. The Zanders had few decorations but they had a big Christmas table with a centerpiece and Swedish ribbon running diagonally from corner to corner. One Christmas here in Minnesota, I saw tables like these at the Swedish Institute.

Pop went shopping in a Swedish deli and made

a big bowl of fish as an appetizer on Swedish ryevita. He had cheeses. He made Swedish appetizers and was allowed to have a bar with drinks out until after Boxing Day. Mum would tell him to leave room for the turkey.

There were little red elves around the centerpiece, called Yule Tomta. Pop was not good at explaining these traditions. But I learned about them later here in Minnesota. And there was a song we sang. It must sound like pigeon Swedish. We did not really know how to pronounce the words- coming up with nonsense syllables like 'Ou Te toot sandior' instead of May you live one hundred years. I have since heard the song sung in Minnesota and have heard it on a record. Christmases came, and I grew older. I watched my older half-brother John Zander bring his girlfriends and then his wife and then-wife and children. And we sang a song.

Then in 1969, Pop died. I flew home for the funeral and stayed for Christmas. We tried to have Christmas for my mother like the old times. I helped her wash the chandelier. She set the table decorations with a Swedish ribbon. There came a point in the dinner when I realized it was time for the song. Who would sing it? John did not seem ready to do it. Maybe this was the beginning of me understanding anthropology and the importance of cultural traditions. I got to my feet like Pop and tapped on a glass for quiet then said like he always did: Well, boys and girls, Ya more da livra! I used the corrected translation. May you live one hundred years! We sang the song. At the end, we all raised our glasses and said louder than all the Vikings fans, a resounding "SKOL!"

There were a few weird things about my own behavior that I want to share. When I first found out I was adopted, my world exploded. I was unhappy. I told myself a story. All this pain does not matter. I am not really from this planet. I am from Jupiter. One day I would leave. My real parents would come and take me back home. This was long before I ever heard the story of Superman from the planet Krypton. I never told anyone this story. It seems I found an archetypal story to help me cope with real-life here. At about 13 years of age, you would see me doing strange turns around in a room. I imagined I needed a thread leading back out to the front door, and I must not get tangled up in this house. So, I turned to keep it untangled.

I ran away from the Zander house a couple of times. One rainy, cold night, I made it all the way down on buses to Chessington Zoo. Maybe my final emigration also falls under this. I escaped left England away from all that crazy emotional tug of war so I could form my own identity. As you can see, I have what has been described as a vivid imagination. All this has affected me positively. I became an anthropologist and help people tell their stories. I also collect fairy tales and folklore.

My main purpose in telling my story is to share with adopted kids some of the weird thoughts I had in trying to understand my identity as an adopted kid. In moving from family to family, as a foster and adopted child, I experienced different family traditions. I want to share with adopted teenagers things I went through emotionally so they might not feel isolated. You are not alone. My hope in sharing this is that adopted teenagers might not feel so alone if you have similar thoughts and behaviors. For me, it was all part of an attempt to sort things out emotionally.

A conflict over class and political identity:

I think one of the biggest issues for foster and adopted kids is identity, social, economic, and cultural identity. In my story, growing up in England, one question is what class did I belong to? Upper, middle, or lower class. Growing up with the Smiths shaped my political attitudes. The Smiths were working-class, blue-collar, Jim worked in construction and then for HMV records. Harry Zander was middle class. Pop was a civil servant, a white-collar. I liked both these men. Pop was a kind man. I have good memories of both these fathers. Knowing the working-class culture, I saw the struggles, the exploitation of workers, and poverty. This influenced me to vote as a democrat. Pop was a conservative.

CHAPTER 15

The Accident

By Leif Wallin

I am at a party making small talk with the cute girls, and I run my fingers through my hair. "Ya know, I have the exact same cowlick as Hugh Grant. I was adopted so that we could be brothers." When things weren't going so well for Hugh, I had to change tactics. Mum Willem Dafoe, yeah, that's the guy, same as Willem Dafoe!

Invariably the women, with best of intentions, would say, "You were adopted? Did you ever find your real parents?"

That always chapped me. I know my *real*

parents. My real parents are the ones who raised me. What should I call them, my fake parents?

My parents did it the right way. They made me feel special. They told me they went to the hospital. They looked for the brightest, happiest, cutest, and voila, that was me!

Eventually, I met other adoptees. I learned that many have a black hole in the soul. They feel something is missing until they find a reason why they'd been surrendered, let go, given up, or other various phrases that are used for adoption. But not me. I was curious about my biological past but was quite happy with the family who chose me. I didn't have that empty feeling. But life changes. I grew up, got married, and we had children, My little daughter, sweet cute little girl. Just yesterday, she was a baby. Then she learned to walk, ride a bike, first date, graduation, off to college. When did "just yesterday" turn into 18 years ago? We were so proud when we dropped her off at college, such a defining moment of parenthood. Then I realized that somewhere out there, I have a birth mom. With me, she had only one defining moment, my birth, and then I was gone. Maybe she is in pain? Maybe she always wonders? If I search, maybe I can put her at ease.

I contacted the adoption agency. They have the files and will search for the mother. This wasn't one of the long, drawn-out searches I had heard about. Just four weeks later, the agency called.

"Leif sit down. We found her. She was from Great Falls, Montana. Her name was Sandy."

I thought it odd that they were speaking in the past tense.

"She died five years ago, but after you, she got married and had three kids, and those children would like to meet you."

Holy smokes what a revelation. In the space of a few minutes, I found and lost a mom and gained three siblings. The new siblings were astonished because I was a secret. Mom had never told them! When they got the call from the agency, they thought it was a practical joke. Think about it, some agency calls and says, your mom had another kid, she just forgot to tell you, for the rest of her life.

I met with my new siblings, and we shared information. Sandy had died five years prior, at age 68 of emphysema. They said that meeting me was like bringing back a piece of their mom. And me, I will always wonder what would have happened if I had searched just a few years earlier.

After processing all this information, I went back and asked the agency about a father search. But they said they could only do a search for the Mother. For the father, they are limited to providing the non-identifying information. I received a package and carefully read it. The file stated that the father was 25 when I was born, of Polish descent, and a high school teacher. I imagined a bureaucrat reading the file with all the information and deciding what information to leave in and what to take out. Hmm, we can tell him this, but not that. I read the file and knew right away that there just wasn't enough information to do a search on my own.

As my new-found siblings shared news of their new brother, friends of the mom, Sandy, would call me or write me letters. I would ask about Sandy's interests, her personality. I received glowing responses, but none knew any information about the father. Then one of Sandy's best friends came through with a crucial piece of information. She told me that all she knew of the father is that he was a minor league baseball player.

Boom! That information filled in a piece of the puzzle. I knew he was 25 when I was born, and with the minor league baseball player clue from the friend, I went to work. Google took me to Baseball.com. It has rosters of every minor league team, names, and important for my search, ages of the players. So now I had to make some assumptions. If Mom was from Great Falls Montana, maybe the man was playing baseball in Great Falls. There it is, the Great Falls Electrics, a minor league team for the Brooklyn Dodgers.

Given that he was a teacher when I was born, I figured he might have been 24 on the 1959 team or 23 on the 1958 team. I filtered out names of 8 "suspects" who would have been 25 the year I was born. I'd google a name, and sometimes I'd find a phone number or an address, but there were a few complete strikeouts, such as no information whatsoever. I'd send an email or make a call. None of the suspects remembered Sandy. I got down to the last name on the list, Joe B. I Google it and get a phone number...I dial the number, a man answers. I can't ask, "Are you my daddy?" so I tell him that I am doing a family history search for Sandy Peterson, and I have learned that she was in a tight relationship with someone on the Great Falls Electrics.

He said, "Sorry, but I don't remember much of that time. I had a stroke and a brain bleed."

Now I feel bad. I wonder how my little treasure hunt has inflicted stress on the men I contacted. I apologize and let him hang up the phone.

But one last effort. I send a letter with a written apology. But I also include the names of three players who I had not been able to find. I ask that if has the contact info of any of these other folks, to let me know.

Two weeks later I get a phone call from Joe. He

admits he had a summer affair with her. She got pregnant about the time the season ended. They went to counseling, and a priest advised that marriage on this basis would not be wise. (Although I wondered that since he was Catholic and she was Lutheran if religion played a role in his advice.) They decided on the adoption. He went back home and never heard from her again. He didn't know she passed away, didn't know if I was a boy or girl, didn't even know my birthday.

We had a nice chat, but as we finished the call, he asked that I not contact anyone else in his family. He since married and has four kids and doesn't want anyone else to know of his little accident, me, even though that was some 50 years ago. Family, certainly, they come in many variations, and they change over time. I grew up with two siblings, a bro, and a sis. Now I have 9, the original 2, 3 more from Sandy, and four who have no clue I exist. There is plenty of love to go around, but you have to open the door.

CHAPTER 16

Patti

By Mary (Marge) Smith

When we moved to Oklahoma City in September of 1962, it was to a rental, and we soon began our search for a home to buy. We found few four-bedroom units available, and eventually, we decided to build. We chose a lot in the city of The Village, a suburb, because of proximity to a YMCA and the Village pool. We moved to my dream home in June of 1964. Martha was in junior high while Chuck and twins Pam and Peggy were in elementary school.

Patti is the adoptive sister of Mike, who was Martha's first boyfriend. He was a foster child in the home of Harold and Lela Hartman, a childless couple. Upon deciding to adopt him legally, they searched for a younger girl to complete their family. They chose Patti, who is native American, through Catholic Charities in Oklahoma City, and the two were adopted together. Patti directly from St. Joseph's Orphanage, where Mike had previously lived. They had not known one another until they became members of the same family.

By the time we met Mike in 1965, the Hartman's had divorced, and Harold resided in Alaska. Lela and the children lived in the family home, a short distance from ours. As a single mom, Lela was employed full time.

Though Mike and Martha were both dating others, they kept in touch. Lured by educational benefits, Mike enlisted in the Air Force upon graduating high school. With no older sibling in the household, Martha frequently looked after Patti on week-ends, and she began spending time at our home. She and Chuck were in the same homeroom at Hoover Junior High, and our entire family grew fond of her.

Summers, Patti, Pam, and Peggy, virtually lived at the Village pool, and Patti gradually spent more time with us. As Lela and I became friends, I became aware of her drinking problem.

Martha wed Tom Weaver in April of 1969. He was in the military and would soon be deployed to Germany. She joined him there prior to our move to Minnesota in August of that year.

I felt like we were leaving Patti behind. She came for a visit the following summer, returning home in time for her birthday, August 21st. A week later, I received a letter from her asking if she could come back and go to school. My husband, Roy, was concerned about responsibility while I was all for it. We put it to a family vote. The ayes had it, Lela was willing, and Patti arrived back in time to start school in September.

As a military dependent, Martha was rotated back to the U.S. ahead of Tom. We looked forward to her visit in January of 1971. Shortly after her arrival, she announced the end of her marriage and settled in. Sometime in February, she tearfully informed me that Patti was pregnant. I was shocked. The physician we consulted referred me to Catholic Charities in Minneapolis, who provided medical care for Patti and counseling for her and the young father, Forrest Janson. He and Chuck were close friends. Roy took the news well, and Lela seemed grateful that I was managing the situation.

Early on, Patti planned to place the baby for adoption and return to Oklahoma. Forrest was adamant that he would not inform his parents. On her advice, I relied on the social worker from Catholic Charities to resolve the issue. Once this was accomplished, I began to communicate with his mom. Her main concern was that Patti have a healthy baby. I am grateful that Gerry and I kept cool heads through the rest of Patti's pregnancy.

I wish that I could have prevented the friction that developed between Forrest, Patti, and Martha. It resulted in Patti leaving our home. I did not know where she was staying, and I had to rely on Chuck's assurance that she was safe and well.

Everything changed on August 24th, when Jennifer Jean arrived. The young couple decided to marry. The next evening, we visited Patti in the hospital, as a family, and healing of the rift began.

Through social services, Patti, as a single mom, was provided with a North Minneapolis apartment. For safety's sake, Forrest was permitted to live there. When they were sure he was committed, his parents consented to his underage marriage. Wisely, Forrest planned to enter the military for educational benefits. By the time he was inducted, the young family was living in the lower level of his parents' home. Another wise decision. Patti has told me many times that she learned a great deal from Gerry, her mother in law.

Meanwhile, Martha completed a business course and was once again out of the nest. We set up a crib in Pam's room, and until they joined

Forrest in California, Patti and Jennifer spent week-ends with us. When he was deployed overseas, the arrangement resumed. Patti obtained her GED and began working at Norwest Bank. As she approaches retirement, she remains with Wells Fargo.

Their marriage lasted ten years. The divorce was amicable, and Forrest and his parents maintain close ties with Jennifer and her family.

Meanwhile, Peggy married and was living in Detroit. She too divorced, and for a time lived with Chuck in his home in Maple Grove, along with daughter Jill. When they moved on, Patti and Jennifer moved in with Chuck, who was single. Patti stayed on as a roommate when Jennifer left home.

By the early '90s, access to adoption records eased, and Patti began her search for her birth family. She was unaware that Lela's dad had registered her with the Indian Nation in Anadarko, Oklahoma. A friend phoned there, on her behalf, on a Sunday afternoon in November, and Patti spoke with an uncle that very evening. Two months later, she and Jennifer attended a reunion, where they met three of Patti's siblings, her mother, and other relatives. They had been searching for Patti, as well. Teresa, the youngest, had not yet been located. The five are half Kiowa and half Oglala Sioux. Teresa was registered as Sioux, and the others as Kiowas, which delayed research.

Chuck lost his right leg below the knee to diabetes and was in danger of losing his home. In 2007, I sold my townhouse, paid off his mortgage, and moved in. The arrangement worked out well. I was comfortable in the lower level of the split entry style house, and changes in their lifestyle were few.

Chuck died suddenly in September of 2014, and I began to make plans for selling the house. As I investigated senior housing options, Patti considered apartments in Maple Grove. I purchased a small townhouse in Maple Grove, and she settled in Coon Rapids near Jennifer's family. We moved in June of 2015. We see one another frequently, especially since Pam and Peggy moved in together in Maple Grove. We hope she will find retirement housing in our area.

If we had it to do over, would we invite Patti into our family? In a heartbeat. We got more than we gave.

CHAPTER 17

Meant to Be

By Christopher Luehr

I was not destined to be a father. As I entered my pre-middle-age, swiftly followed by my early middle-age and then solidly middle age, I saw more of my friends becoming parents and seeming to love it. My best friend couldn't wait to get married and start a family. A good law school friend once told me that he was "born to be a father."

Meanwhile, my life was still filled with late nights, sleepy Saturdays, and a plethora of hobbies. And by in large, that was just fine with me. Children meant no fun and no freedom. Essentially, they meant no Me. What I forgot in those youthful calculations of my pre-middle age was that Me was always changing.

Part of the life of my bachelorhood was exploring the world of internet-suggested dates. Some were fun. Some were boring. All of them ultimately ended with me alone. One such date changed my life, though I didn't know it at the time.

A series of very fortunate events, a forward-thinking algorithm, and the wise hand of God blinked a message on my phone one day in late summer. "You have a match!" I felt the thrill of a potential date, someone to walk with around Lake of the Isles, and perhaps steal a sweet kiss from under the harvest moon. But first, I had to put her through my time-tested gauntlet of pre-date questions. I was a busy guy and didn't have time to waste on dead-end dates.

So, I asked her the standard questions you ask when starting an app-based romance in the modern age: Where are you from? What's your favorite movie? How much student debt do you have? You know, the basics.

Also, as a man in pre and early middle-age with baby showers scattered across my calendar, I also asked this mystery woman, "Do you have any kids?"

"Kinda," she replied. Of all the potential answers, this was not one I expected.

As it turns out, this amazing woman was a single foster mother who had assisted five children in reuniting with their birth parents. So sometimes she had kids, sometimes she didn't. At the time, she had two toddlers, both of them hoping to reunite with their birth parents eventually.

Here is where the mystery of God's ways started to work in my life. If she had already been a permanent mother, I might have balked. I would have gone on a date or two, surely, just to prove to myself and the world that I was open-minded enough to take on such a situation. I was strong; I was cool. I was mature. But ultimately, I might have buckled under the pressure of having to raise children, especially those not my own. That would be far too complicated for the simple, free life I had planned for myself.

Alternatively, if there had been no children in the picture, and romance did blossom into more, I might have fought to maintain the status quo and resist discussions about bringing children into the mix. But fostering? That seemed to be the best of both worlds.

At that point, I fancied myself a "fun uncle" despite having no biological nieces or nephews. I loved to play and joke and have fun with kids, so long as they were someone else's kids. Sometimes I was expending the kiddos' energy and helping prepare them for naptime or bedtime. Other times, I wound them up only to disappear back into the fog of my single life, leaving the parents to corral the bouncing ball of a child I left behind. Never intentionally, of course. I always thought I was helping because who doesn't like to have fun? I certainly did and had as much as possible. That meant I was a great play partner, but not ready to be a great parent.

Whenever a wet or messy diaper arose, or a funny face or bear hug did not quickly quell the crying, that cued my time exit. Fun Uncle Chris was here for the good times, but not for a long time. I was like a kid who eats the frosting off cupcakes and then leaves the rest for whoever cleans up defrosted cupcakes (parents. I now know the answer is parents clean and sometimes eat defrosted cupcakes).

And that was enough for me, and for many of my friends. They enjoyed having an adult friend stop by, and any distraction I provided was a welcome respite for mom and dad, too. So, I thought that was my role. Fun uncle for life!

But then I learned of fostering. "Great!" thought my ego. "This is like Fun Uncle PLUS social cred!" I would get to be the father of the kiddos but then send them back to bio-mom and bio-dad after a short vacation with Fun Uncle Chris. Sure, there would be more messy diapers, and I would have to stick around through crying fits and midnight feedings, but ultimately, I would still be "free." Parenthood was FOREVER, and I didn't think I was ready for that.

So, for a few months, I was a foster father with my girlfriend and our/her foster daughter. And it was great. I learned to love a bit more. The little bundles of joy and screams and poop began to crack open deeper caverns of emotion that I'd papered over with now juvenile distractions, like parties, whole days spent reading/napping, or YouTube rabbit holes. Slowly, I became too busy or tired or invested (all three seemed to happen at once) I couldn't focus solely on my personal goals. They were admirable for sure: lose that last 100 pounds, build a business, or write a brilliant book. Those seemed rather small compared to the pleasure our foster daughter received from a short round of peek-a-boo or playing "what sounds does this animal make?"

Foster fatherhood felt good. My girlfriend and I got into a good rhythm. In the morning, I'd drop the kiddo off at daycare; then she would pick her up after work. And since we weren't living together at the time, I would be able to head back to my apartment for a few nights and play bachelor, which mostly consisted of noshing too much junk food and watching endless internet videos. But all at my own pace, in my own space, with loads of quiet.

For the most part, we were rehearsing family life pretty well. Splitting diaper duties, tag-teaming feedings, and loads of group family fun. Honestly, she was taking the lion's (and tiger's and bear's) share as the official foster mom, but again, God was easing me into the fatherhood role at the appropriate pace. First, a couple of days a week. Then three, four, until I was no longer the boyfriend of foster parents. I became a foster parent myself. The little girl was no longer her foster daughter. She was *our* foster daughter.

We also juggled unusual parental tasks of monitoring weekly bio-parent visits, occasional drop-ins by the social worker or guardian ad litem, and monthly court visits to check on the bioparents' progress with the judge's outline plan. Often with children placed in foster care, the court sets out a plan of action for the parent(s) to follow in order to achieve reunification. As I mentioned, my lady had already shepherded five children through weeks or months of foster care back to successful reunification with their family. We had no reason to think anything would be different from our current foster daughter.

Until things got different. About eight months into our relationship, my girlfriend, toddler foster daughter, and I learned that her bio-mom wasn't complying with the court-ordered plan. It was heartbreaking, especially for my girlfriend. She championed all bio-parents and gave them buckets of grace as they fought to get back on their feet. Some in the foster community and beyond demonize these folks as "bad" people or "negligent" parents. My girlfriend took a different approach, choosing instead to view their transgressions with sympathy and family restoration as the chief objective. But there comes a point when sympathy and second chances become damaging to the future of the child, the preservation of which is the ultimate goal of everyone involved. Despite the best efforts of everyone involved, it became clear that our foster daughter wouldn't be reunited with her bio-parents.

The next step is to look at the extended family to find someone who might be willing and able to provide permanent care. But no viable candidates appeared there either. So, slowly but suddenly, my girlfriend and I began the discussion about adopting our little wonder. Usually, couples discuss their first road trip or moving in together or marriage before they talk about adopting a child. But our relationship never followed the usual pattern. Our first big decision carried a weight that would reverberate through the rest of our lives.

Though I would like to say that I threw open my heart and embraced the idea of adoption as soon as it was placed on the table. But frankly, I was thrown by the prospect. Despite enjoying foster fatherhood, at least most of it (no one really enjoys a 3 am soothing fest on a Monday night), this step felt much bigger. The distinction seems small on paper. Foster father—>adoptive father. But the chasm looked large to me, and one I wasn't sure I could cross.

I made pros and cons lists in my head. Pro: I get this wonderful family in my life and will watch our girl grow up into an amazing adult. Con: I am responsible for this person, emotionally, financially, spiritually, and every way FOREVER. Pro: I have an incredible partner who seems to know a lot about this parenting stuff and is willing to coach me along the way. Con: It's crazy to consider such a commitment with a woman I've known less than a year. It seemed daunting, especially as I still felt I was a major work in progress. How could I care for someone else when I was barely keeping all my plates spinning? I still had figure a few things out, and I was already passing through early-middle with alarming speed (I was 38 at the time, which some might even consider actual middle age). Was I too immature to care for a child? Was I too old to be a first-time dad? I went back and forth with these questions in my head each day, placing a new tally mark on each side. I also volleyed these concerns back and forth with my girlfriend, who had swiftly landed on the pro-adoption side. She did have a couple of questions early on but was much faster to commit to the little girl who had been in her care since she was three days old than I was. She and I had discussions and arguments. Some cool-headed, and others tear-filled. I didn't want to let her down, but I didn't want to make a huge life-decision just to spare the feelings of a girlfriend, though, in my heart of hearts, I knew she was already much more than that.

And therein lie the answer to making this decision: I stopped thinking about it.

For an overly-educated man like myself, pressing pause on my brain was no small task. Everything I'd accomplished, places I had visited, choices I had made had come from my big ole brain. And many of them had worked out pretty well. But that tool was failing me now. Because a decision to create a family can't be made by following an equation. You make it by following something deeper, more mysterious, and more powerful. Becoming a parent is not a brain-decision. It's a heart decision.

From this vantage point, I saw my life had been leading me to this place. From becoming a meditator to overcoming shyness to learning personal financial health to becoming a renewed Christian to taking better care of my health...all the strands of my life wove a crooked but clear path to that moment. Apparently, unrelated choices and nudges lead me to the place where I could even ask, "Can I be a father?" Or, more to the point, "Can I be *this child's* father?"

Once I allowed the pros and cons to fade away, and when I permitted the gravity and levity and challenge and joy of this decision wash over my heart, the choice became clear. I was meant to be her father, and we were meant to form this family. It wasn't the family I had pictured in my head as a 17-year-old or 23-year-old, or even a 38-year-old. By as a 40-year-old man firmly in middle age and firmly standing in my own heart, I saw this was the family I was destined to have.

So, months before we were engaged and nearly a year before we were married, my girlfriend and I decided to move forward with adoption.

Her adoption came first because of her foster background. The day after I turned forty, with the courtroom packed with family, friends, social workers, and importantly, our daughter's bio-mother and two brothers, I sat next to my then fiancé while the judge finalized her adoption. The room was bursting with love, and it was a glorious celebration of our journey. Over two years after she'd brought that little girl home from the hospital, she became her legal mother.

After our wedding, a couple of months later, I went through the official adoption process myself. My adoption date just included me, my then-wife, our daughter, and my mother. A smaller, simpler affair, but the courtroom was no less bursting with love than it had been six months earlier. That day we walked out of the courtroom with papers that matched the family we had formed in our hearts. At one point in my life, I didn't know if I was meant to be a father, but after the judge proclaimed us dad and daughter, I couldn't imagine my life any other way. Our beautiful, complicated journey to adoption was finally over, and our wonderful adventure as a family was just beginning.

A Baby Is A Miracle

Author Unknown

This little tiny baby,
Was sent from God above,
To fill our hearts with happiness,
And touch our lives with love,
He must have known,
We'd give our all,
And always do our best.
To give our precious baby love,
And be grateful and so blessed.

CHAPTER 18

A German Girl in Our Lives

By John Strahan

This is a story that I have told more than once and am willing to tell it to anyone who will listen. Without fail, it brings tears to my eyes and warmth to my heart. I gladly respond to Dianne Rowe's request to share our story. It is over 53 years old but still worth telling.

We were married in August 1962 in Minnesota and currently living in Germany when we thought it was a good time to begin having a family. Barbara had a miscarriage, and the doctor thought that we should not have children ourselves because of potential heart problems

from   childhood   rheumatic   fever.
Disappointment was short-lived, and we decided
to adopt a child. We were in Germany because
John had been assigned there while in the Air
Force. US military personnel had an easier path
to follow because we did not have to wait until
we had demonstrated we could not parent
children on our own. This meant Germans were
often in their 40's before they could begin an
adoption process. We were in our late 20's and
considered to be excellent candidates.

In 1966, we visited the City Youth Office in
Würzburg and spoke with Frau Pickle about our
desire. This office had jurisdiction over children
placed in orphanages. We had to pay $25.00 for
the cost of the background investigation on both
of us. Aside from the $25.00 fee for a visa for Elke
to travel to the US, that was the only expense we
ever paid in the adoption process. In response to
her questions, we told Frau Pickle that we wanted
a boy because we thought that would be a nice
way to begin a family, wanted a white child
because we were not sure we could handle the
issues of the child of a black GI and white German
girl, and we wanted a Protestant because we
would not agree to raise a child as a Catholic; we
were living in the Catholic State of Bavaria. She
noted our desires and told us to visit the
orphanages in the area to find a child who would
meet our expectations. Once that had been done,

we could proceed to the next steps.

The unit that John was assigned to sponsored a Christmas celebration at an orphanage near our base. We thought that would be a good place to begin. There was a 2-year-old boy with long blonde hair and a name we would have changed living there. The operator of the orphanage said she thought she could find the birth mother to sign the necessary papers if we paid what she owed. We said that we did not intend to "buy a baby." That meant he was no longer a possibility for us. In hindsight, this lack of willingness on our part likely played a role in our inability to find a child.

Additionally, orphanages were receiving fewer children because abortion was becoming more common, and birth parents were not meeting their financial obligations. Third parties could pay the bill if they chose to do so. Neither the City Youth Office, nor we found another candidate for potential adoption.

On Tuesday, June 28, 1966, we returned to Frau Pickle's office to tell her we had to stop looking because we were returning to the States in late October of the same year. She told us the problem was that we insisted upon having a boy. We said that was not exactly true – we would have accepted a three-legged cat! We did not intentionally exclude girls from consideration, and we were sorry if we had left that impression.

To her, that made a great deal of difference. She scrawled something on a piece of paper and told us to go to a specific address in Würzburg of an orphanage operated by order of Lutheran nuns, show them this note as a girl there might be available to us. We uttered a "Yes Mam" and looked forward with great anticipation as to what might happen on Thursday. We might finally be on a track that we sought.

(Anecdote: As I write this, we have a grand-cat who is three-legged. Quinnley Jo stays with us when she comes to visit from Arizona. She lost a rear leg in an accident and was at a local ASPCA facility when our granddaughter brought her into her orbit. She stays with us because another cat lives in the other house. It took over 50 years, but we did finally receive what we were willing to accept! I must also let you know that we no longer have possession of the large stack of paperwork generated in the entire adoption, immigration, and naturalization process. It was given to Elke when she was married in April 1992. Hence, some specific dates and building names may no longer be accurately remembered, but the events are firmly planted in my heart and mind.)

When we returned to our apartment, our landlady, Pia, and her mother, Oma, wanted a full report on what had happened. We excitedly told them. We also learned that city social welfare people had visited the house to inspect and determine whether or not it was suitable for a prospective adoptive child. Pia and Oma were slightly insulted by this but also knew it was important if we were to have any success. They and the house had been approved! They anticipated the events of Thursday as much as we did. We had made no preparations, either physical or mental, for the addition of a child to our household. We did imagine that on Thursday, we might need to address these concerns. We would take one step at a time and deal with it as appropriate. Do not get excited until it is proper to do so!

On Thursday, June 30, 1966, as instructed, we appeared at the orphanage, which was near the main train station in Würzburg. We passed to the office staff the note Frau Pickle had given us. The people knew who we were and why we were there, and they were prepared to do as instructed. The City Youth Office had jurisdiction over kids in the orphanage. We were not allowed to enter the residential areas of the orphanage. We waited while someone went to get the child of our focus. Soon one of the nuns appeared on the stairway.

The child in her arms was one year and four days old. She was wearing a white bonnet, dark blue sweater, and what appeared to be pink leggings and oversized shoes. One gaze and both my heart and my mind said, "Oh my gosh, this is my daughter!"

Of course, first, a process had to be followed - a physical examination to be certain she could qualify to immigrate to the United States. Something like TB would halt that possibility. Elke Kramer was placed in Barbara's arms. Her life was surrounded by women, and she was more comfortable with them. We took her to the US Army Hospital and said we were considering adopting this child and needed to know if there was anything wrong with her that would preclude doing that and returning to the United States. Following their examination, we were told that she did not have TB, and there was no other reason why she would not be admitted to the United States under the appropriate visa. What a relief!

I do not recall how long we had Elke that day and what we did aside from the physical examination. The orphanage expected that we would return her, and we did.

On the same day, we returned to Frau Pickle's office and told her that we had confirmed there was no medical reason why she could not immigrate to the US, and we wanted to adopt Elke. She asked if we wanted to bring her home the next day, and we said that was not possible because we had made absolutely no preparations to accommodate her. We asked if Monday of the next week would be OK, and she affirmed that it would be so we operated on that basis.

When we returned home, we passed the good news to Pia and Oma. Elke was about to enter a home where she would acquire both an Aunt and a Grandmother as well as a set of parents. We borrowed a crib from the nursery at the chapel where I was assigned, and a gleeful couple from the base loaned us their fold-up highchair. We bought a stroller with an attached umbrella and underneath storage area. Elke could ride in it as well as have a place to sleep when we made trips.

We bought clothes that we thought were appropriate in size (they were too small) because we could not bring her home in clothes from the orphanage. We acquired 12 diapers with rubber pants because that was enough (this was also wrong), and bottles for water, milk, and juice were needed and acquired. It took us only three days to be ready to be parents, not nine months! Where there is a will, there is a way!

On Monday, July 4, 1966, we returned to the City Youth Office. From Frau Pickle, we received a document certifying that Elke was to be in our custody because we were going to adopt her. This document needed to be with us at all times lest some authority think we were stealing a child to sell across the border. We faced this question on a trip where we left Germany, entered Austria for a short distance, and returned to Germany. We also received the signed and notarized authorization from the birth mother that we could take Elke to the US for adoption purposes. We also had to deal with the issue that documents had to be in both German and English. Certified copies were acquired as needed.

At the orphanage, we were not allowed to go to the nursery to see where Elke had lived and prepare her for entering our family. The nuns were absolutely appalled that pins would be used to hold diapers in place. Only the rubber pants were used for that purpose. The clothes we brought were used, and we soon left the building with a list of other things to do. The staff at the orphanage were not happy that Americans were going to take Elke. They had no choice in the matter.

One of the first pictures of Elke was taken so we could obtain a passport for her. We had planned a trip to Denmark and Sweden, and she, of course, would go with us. This is that picture.

ELKE ON THE DAY SHE CAME HOME WITH US.

Once the Passport issue had been resolved, we

had to get clothes that fit as well as the kind of food that Elke was eating while in the orphanage. It looked like cream of wheat and was consumed through a large hole in the nipple on the bottle. Once she discovered other food, she quickly rejected the old stuff.

Our good friend, Elizabeth, had gone with us to the orphanage. She was a mother, fluent in English, and could learn from the orphanage the kind of information we needed to make Elke's transition smooth. We brought Elke home on July 4, 1966. An Independence Day celebration was held at our base, and we went and strutted our stuff.

Pushing the stroller is her daughter, Diane. We do not remember either the name or function of the young woman in the background. Of course, Mother Barbara carries a diaper bag! My military unit got to meet our daughter. Women held a Baby Shower for Barbara at the NCO Club on the base.

Barbara had been working as an educational assistant at the base where I was stationed. She had to give a two-week notice to leave her job. During this time, Elke was with different babysitters during the day. She accepted us at the end of the day as the appropriate people to be with. In our apartment, Elke had her crib in our bedroom, and she slept well. She liked it when we changed her diapers because that had been a playtime in the orphanage. She quickly observed that we were not eating the same thing she was and she wanted to share with us. (Obviously, a thoughtful child!) She was not in the hallway connecting our rooms much because it was also a stairwell from one floor to the next. In the early days, she would not play on the carpet in our living room. She had come from the nursery were babies did not play on carpeted floors. Grass was in the same category but, eventually, both surfaces were acceptable to her. In the early days, she was suspicious of men so it took a while for her to discover she could wrap me around her finger. I threw her in the air once, and a screaming and bawling child landed in my arms. I did not do that again. Both Pia and Oma loved this child, who was now in their home. Often, they were willing to watch her as we did something else. Banging her hands on their piano was especially fun.

In the mid-1960s, Europeans did not take their small children with them when they traveled. On the other hand, Americans did! We had a Volkswagen Microbus, and I removed the center seat to create an area for Elke. Her stroller was used as a nap area. The fold-up highchair could be extended and become a place where she could eat. A woolen blanket on the floor was a great play area. As required, Barbara could get into this area through the opening between our seats to do whatever had to be done. When we stopped for a meal, we were confronted with anger in restaurants who did not appreciate us using our fold up highchair into their establishment. There was no such thing as a "child menu," so Barbara tended to select food that she could share with Elke. Finding a place to sleep was never a problem – we just went to bed earlier! While on a ferry from Germany to Denmark, I inquired of myself: What have we done?

Because I had not been in the military service for six years, we had to pay for the return of Barbara and Elke to the United States. In October 1966, they flew from Frankfurt, Germany to Detroit, Michigan, where they stayed with my mother and grandfather until I arrived. I flew later to McGuire Air Force Base, where I was discharged from the Air Force on October 26th. I had served five years, 11 months, and 26 days on active duty. I went to the port in New Jersey, where our car had been shipped. With it in hand, I drove to Detroit to get my wife and daughter as well as visit with my family. After a few days, we headed for Minnesota, where we intended to begin a new life. We finally arrived at the farm, and Elke could meet her new grandparents. Her grandfather came from the barn where he had been milking cows – he apparently smelled funny because she did not immediately embrace him. Staying with Barbara's parents on the farm gave us a firm and stable setting so we could now do something else.

We had not completed the adoption of Elke in Germany because there was not enough time to do so. We had to register her presence with us with local social services people. They could not remove her from us unless she was abused. The social worker who came to our apartment wondered why this 16-month old child did not speak German. My brother Tom, an attorney in the Twin Cities area, offered to handle the adoption for us. That took a large area of concern from us, and we appreciated it very much. He met the expense of the process. It was a complicated thing because everything needed to be in two languages and passed through many hands until arriving at a specific action point in two countries. Our former landlady, Pia, worked in the registrar office of the local court system, would watch for anything on our case and see that it was handled as rapidly as possible. I do not recall when the adoption was finalized, but I am certain that Elke has that information in the pile of paper that we gave to her. The adoption was completed before we could address the naturalization process.

Once major issues are resolved, any adopted

child just fades into the background like any other child. We moved to Cedar Rapids, bought our first house, and settled as any family would. Elke acquired a brother in October 1967, and we likely had a dog as a pet. She did not like her name because it was different and eventually discovered that a unique name can be helpful. There was one more important thing to do.

When Elke entered the United States in October 1966, she came under a program where she was to be adopted and, when appropriate, would become a naturalized citizen. As a child, she did not have to pass through some kind of citizenship course and test process, and she did not. On April 22, 1970, in a court in Cedar Rapids, she became a US citizen. She was one of three children that day.

—Gazette photo by John McIvor

Youngest New Citizens

Three Cedar Rapids youngsters were among 42 persons who became citizens of the United States in naturalization ceremonies Tuesday before Judge Edward J. McManus. From left are Maria Elena Dean, 5, Peter Manuel Dean, 4, and Elke Lynn Strahan, 4. The Dean youngsters, children of Mr. and Mrs. Ernest S. Dean, jr., 325 Brentwood drive NE, are natives of Costa Rica. Miss Strahan's parents are Mr. and Mrs. John R. Strahan, 216 Broadmore road NW. She is a native of Germany. July 4 will be an even bigger big day for Elke Strahan now that she is a citizen. She was born on Independence day.

This article appeared in the Cedar Rapids Gazette of April 22, 1970. The text included an error: she entered our home on July 4th but was born on June 26th. At this ceremony, she received her Certificate, and it has been preserved in a safe place so that she could vote and later acquire a passport for foreign travel. One of my co-workers had also been transferred to Cedar Rapids when I was, and he and his wife were witnesses who knew me for more than two years which the court required. Elke remembers her Naturalization – she was four years, ten months old at the time. We celebrated with lunch out, and one of her friends and her brother joined us. Her younger sister was not born until December 1970.

I sit rocking in my chair as I seek to draw a couple of instances of things that happened because Elke was adopted. In her elementary school days, both she and a friend, who was also adopted, were assigned a task to trace their family history. They cried because they could not do the assignment. A suggestion was made to the teacher that she should be aware of such circumstances and phrase the assignment in a different way. She did, and they did the task. In her college years, Elke took a class in German. She did not do well in it. A scientific and clear demonstration that language is learned not installed in DNA.

Elke was married in April 1992. She announced this information well in advance to our former landlady, Pia. Pia and her husband were invited to the wedding, and they both came.

It was especially nice for all of us that this confirmation of her history happened. Elke's roots are Germanic, even though she cannot speak the language.

I will close with this last experience that we had because Elke was adopted. In 1987 we made a trip to Germany and Southern France. Elke was with us for two of the three weeks. One of our objectives was to visit the orphanage in Würzburg, where she had spent the first year of her life. Our landlady, Pia, did not think this was a good idea but she made the arrangements for our visit. The building had been repurposed as a residence for kids with problems. We were shown the room that had been the nursery during Elke's time there. They still had a card in a desk file that showed she had been placed in our custody on July 4, 1966. As we returned to our car, Elke was crying. We asked what the problem was? Her answer was, "It was a nice place." It was a nice place because the people who operated the orphanage loved and cared for the children who had been placed in their custody. They were not happy that "The Americans" took their Elke away but never imagined that someone or something should interrupt the prospect that Elke would have a good life. When we left, we were all crying about the experience we had just shared.

It has been well over 50 years since the adoption was initiated. A great variety of unique policies and procedures have been exercised in the process, and here we are. Most of the drama of an adoption ceased when Elke was naturalized. All of the steps taken mattered because they were necessary to accomplish what we sought – Elke as our daughter. Elke is the oldest of our three children. She is the only one we picked.

CHAPTER 19

No Longer the Eldest

By Dawn McClean

Adoption, particularly years ago, was about keeping skeletons in the closet. I know my family has many skeletons that I don't know about (and some that I do, but have kept quiet about). One of these skeletons was revealed to me when I was 19...when I found out I wasn't my mother's eldest child, but that I was actually a middle child and had a half-brother who was close to a decade older than I was. It was a shock, to say the least.

There I was, just heading out the door to work when Mom mentioned it in passing. Okay. What was I supposed to do with that information?

Suddenly, I had the older brother I'd always wanted, even if it made me a middle child...but yet I was still the oldest and didn't really have an older sibling to look out for me or annoy me, either.

Thinking about it, some things started to make sense. This older brother had a similar birthday to mine, which helped to explain why I have never liked birthdays because mine always ended up in tears and family arguments. I suppose at that time of year, Mom was reminded of the baby she gave up for adoption. Because Dad knew about this, he would know why she was out of sorts, but of course, I knew nothing except that my parents often weren't in good moods, though they did try. Many years on now, and I still get uptight around birthdays (my own and others), because those earlier experiences are ingrained in me.

Mom didn't want to give her son up for adoption but felt she didn't have a choice, being just 19 in the early 60s and in a position where the father was not able to be with her. Mom went away to a different area to a home for unwed mothers during the time leading up to the birth. This, of course, was so that no one in her small-town area would find out that she was pregnant. In fact, I'm not sure Mom's older brother even knew about the pregnancy because he was quite a bit older than Mom, and he was already long out in the world making his own living at that time.

Mom had been looking for a son, Matt, ever since the day she gave him up for adoption. She became an expert in reading between the lines of the non-identifying information that the adoption department sent out in response to questions. For many years she was involved in an adoption group and helped others find their parents or children. She was able to do this for others but wasn't able to find her own son during that time.

Mom's adoption case was made more complicated due to the adoption being completed in another jurisdiction than where it began. Eventually, the rules did change, and she was able to put her name on the register so that should Matt want contact with her, it would be recorded that she was willing.

A couple of years later, Matt also put his name on the list and Social Services contacted Mom to say that he would accept a letter from her through the department. Actually, the call came while my parents were on vacation so I received the exciting call that contact was going to happen. After a few letters, a phone call was arranged between them to chat, and eventually, they would meet.

After having the adoption finalized in a different jurisdiction, my half-brother's family did eventually move back to where it began, just a couple of hours away from where I grew up. Mom did tell her mother that she had met her son, which must have been awkward because back at the time of the adoption, once it was completed, it was never to be spoken of again.

The awkwardness around this birth and adoption continued for me; it's not my position to say anything to anyone about it. But how exactly am I supposed to reply when someone asks if I have any brothers or sisters? "Yes, I have a younger sister, as well as an older half-brother that I've never met?" That's weird. But to leave him out also seems rude and dismissive.

It's very strange to know there's someone out there who has half of the same gene pool as you; that you could pass by in the street and never know it. I might have thought he looked a little familiar for some unknown reason, but to him, I'd be just another face in the crowd.

It's much more common these days to have wider and more complex family units that can be composed of step-parents, step- and half-siblings. There are open adoptions where the families all know each other and stay in touch over the years. Still, it's not my place to divulge this information, even if it has become a part of me.

A few years later, I was able to meet Matt and his wife, Terri, over breakfast with Mom. They were both fun and relaxed, and we seemed to have a similar sense of humor. They have good careers and a family of their own that is close and does a lot together, even now that the children are grown and have lives of their own. I did meet up with them once again when I was in the area with my husband. I'm not sure if their children knew who I was, but I did meet two of them as they passed through the house, busy with their social lives.

Matt reminds me so much of Mom's brother, both in appearance and in demeanor; he's definitely from that side of the family, without a doubt. It's interesting to see nature at work with some things rather than nurture.

For a couple of years, Matt and I exchanged emails once a year or so, but now I only have an email forwarded from Mom every few years. Life gets busy and moves on. I imagine he's now thinking about retirement from his mentally stressful position of keeping the world safe and looking forward to spending more time on his leisure pursuits with Terri and his family.

As I mentioned earlier, this isn't really my story to tell, as the adoption didn't have anything to do with me, and happened long before I arrived on the planet. However, the actions taken a decade before I was born still did affect me and turned my inner world upside down for a while in my 20s. To find out you're not the eldest, where does that put you now?

I am grateful that Matt grew up in a loving and community-minded family and that he is a pillar in his community. I do believe that for everyone involved, the choices made almost 60 years ago have played out well.

There is a Song

BY SPIKE MILLIGAN

There is a song in man
There is a song in woman
And that is the child's song.
When that song comes
There will be no words.
Do not ask where they are.
Just listen to the song.
Listen to it-
Learn it-
It is the greatest song of all

About the Authors

The history of *Adoption Matters* began a long, long time ago...in my mind. I noticed when people learned that you had adopted, they often wanted to know more. They were interested in the story. The why! The baby! Not that you shared. It was just something I noticed.

After retiring from my 40 hour a week job, I now had time to pursue some of my interests, one being writing. I joined the **Maple Grove Senior Writing group** and for years wrote lots of essays. Then one day I noticed from the readings of others in our group how many of the writers had also adopted and some, like us, had biological children too. After pondering this a bit, I asked my fellow writers if anyone was interested in writing a book with our adoption stories. It was well received, and thus began our journey into *Adoption Matters*. Some of the writers are not from our writing group but their beautiful stories are wonderful additions.

How fortunate that we have the opportunity to choose adoption or foster children. We all need love and having choices is such a blessing.

Lois Miller Caswell

Lois Miller Caswell grew up on a big dairy farm five miles west of Osseo, Minnesota. She graduated from Osseo High school and attended Northwestern Hospital School of Nursing and Macalester College. She was almost ready to graduate when the "love bug" bit, and instead of graduating, she married and joined her new husband Earl in the U.S. Air Force for a three-year honeymoon in England. Lois spent 40 years in various areas of the Real Estate field, spending most of her time in new construction. In the meantime, she and Earl raised three wonderful kids and now are enjoying their two grandkids.

Lois is learning to enjoy being retired and having time to write short stories about her life and that of her family. She was privileged to grow up with grandparents next door, so there are lots of stories from those days as well. She and Earl live in Maple Grove, are very active in their church, love to travel, and especially enjoy "Road Trips."

Katie DeCosse

JACKIE MAHER AND KATIE DECOSSE

Katie DeCosse was born and raised in the Minneapolis area. Much of her career was spent in the veterinary world as a technician as well as a Veterinary Technology educator. Spare time is spent reading, rug hooking, knitting, and gardening. In 2009, along with her birth mother, Jackie Maher, she published a book about their reunion experience. (*Fifty Years in 13 days – A Mother/Daughter Reunion*) To this day, they see each other on a regular basis.

Esther and John Holgate

Regarding John and Esther Holgate, adoptive parents of Angela Holgate (Shin Hyun Ok) of South Korea:

(Angela joined the Holgate Family at age 20 months. In 1971. At age 40, she died of cervical cancer Jan. 2009, leaving a 20-month-old son Damon, whom she adopted brother and wife, in turn, have since adopted and are now raising.)

John Holgate, a third adopted child of Bob and Mildred Holgate, was raised in Austin, MN, during the late '30s to mid-'50s. His father was a barber and mother, a seamstress for an interior decorator and salesperson.

Esther Holgate, born in 1937 in Youngstown, Ohio, lived in northern India from ages 8 to 15 as a child of Presbyterian missionaries. She spent school vacations at her missionary aunt's orphanage near Rupaidiha, Uttar Pradesh, India.

John and Esther were married in Corpus Christi, Texas, in 1962. They lived briefly in Aransas Pass, Texas, teaching in the local high school. In 1963 they moved to Lake Crystal, Minnesota, where Esther continued teaching high school French and English while John attended Mankato State University to receive his MS in High School Counseling. Subsequently, he took the position as Lake Crystal High School Counselor for the next 30 years. Esther retired from teaching to care for family and other pre-school children in their home. Six years later, she worked for the next 15 years at a senior care facility in Lake Crystal.

During this time, John and Esther were actively involved in the Episcopal Church in Mankato. They soon added two sons to the family, Robert (b. 1964) and Aaron (b. 1967). Wishing to add a daughter to the family without the natural guess-work and being familiar with the idea of adoption, they began to search adoption agencies for a baby girl. They found there was a long waiting list and not much available locally, so they applied to Minnesota Lutheran Social Services, who were affiliated with an agency bringing Korean orphans to US families. A year and a half later, Shin Hyun Ok arrived from Il San Orphanage, Seoul, South Korea.

Ann Kalin

Ann was born in California, raised in a military family living throughout the United States, and currently lives in Minneapolis for six months and Florida for six months with her husband of 48 years. We are enjoying our retirement playing golf, tennis, and walking the beaches of Southwest Florida. Per my story, we have two adopted children and four grandchildren. Vivian was born in May of 2012, Valentina was born in 2017, and the twins were born December 2018. They bring such joy to our lives.

Ann worked in the computer industry for over thirty years, beginning as a programmer at the Pentagon in Washington D.C., then as a systems analyst for GE Capital and Honeywell on several financial projects in Minnesota. Ann taught computer programming at Hennepin Technical College for eight years when her children were young, which gave her the summers to enjoy her children. Ann founded and was the principal owner of ONYX Software Development Training Company for 18 years, which was sold in 2016 when she retired. ONYX provided onsite training for medium to large companies, such as St. Paul Companies, SuperValu Stores, Federated Mutual Insurance Company, Kimberly Clark, USBank, BI Performance, and Norwest. Ann has her BS in Mathematics from James Madison University in Virginia and graduate-level studies at the University of Maryland and University of Minnesota in Management Information Systems.

Christopher Luehr

Chris Luehr is a storyteller, attorney, professional speaker, coach, dinner-table comedian, and North Minneapolis resident. Born in Cloquet, Minnesota, Chris' first job after college landed him in Northeastern China, the one region in the world with more snow than Minnesota. After a few years of teaching in China, Chris continued his education with a Master's degree in Comparative Literature from Columbia University and a law degree from the University of Minnesota. Whether speaking on a stage, arguing in a courtroom or coaching in a boardroom, Chris enjoys connecting with people and helping them write their next chapter.

Through his organization, Joyful Noize (joyfulnoize.net), he helps mission-driven organizations promote their message through story. He learned the importance of storytelling from his father and carries that message to individuals and companies throughout the Twin Cities and beyond. When not working with business or legal clients, he enjoys making music, cycling, and exploring new adventures. 2019's adventures have included completing his first triathlon, flying trapeze classes, shooting pistols, skydiving, and, best of all, getting married. In addition to the power of a good story, Chris believes in the great healing of a good hug, the unifying energy of laughter, and restorative capabilities of a clean pair of socks.

Jackie Maher

JACKIE MAHER

I first retired from writing at age 8 years. Sister Bernadette challenged us to write a story to be judged by our classmates. I asked myself "what would my readers like to hear about?" I still do that. I decided to write about a fluffy white kitten and walked away with the prize, a miraculous meddle or a holy card, and retired my pencil for another forty-five years. I always made up stories in my head, some of them novel length but never showed them around.

After I had raised my 5 children and sent them to pursue their destinies, I enrolled in classes at North Hennepin Community College. It was there that I discovered that my writing had merit. I chose the genre of the essay because I know a little bit about a lot of things so essays fulfill my urge to write. And I do not have to answer to Kinsey Milhone or Stephanie Plum to keep the ball in the air and what with Steinbeck, Fitzgerald and Hemingway gone, who's going to stop me now?

Dawn McClean

Dawn McClean grew up on the prairies before adventuring to pastures afar. She has a BA (with Honors) in developmental psychology that comes in handy while raising her family. Mom by day, work from home VA by night, Dawn always has a project (or 10) on the go. Her hobbies include reading, writing to friends around the world by slow mail, and various craft endeavors.

Dianne L. Rowe

Dianne Rowe grew up in North Minneapolis when times were pretty innocent. Retired from the corporate world, she has an AA Degree from North Hennepin Community College, lives in Maple Grove, where she is a member of a Senior Writing Group. Writes essays about life as she knows it; Published in *Family Digest* and she just finished writing a children's Christmas picture book. "I find there is a wonderful freedom in writing," she says.

Irene Reuteler

I grew up in the southwest area of Minneapolis, where I was fortunate to have grandparents, aunts, uncles, and cousins nearby and where I met and married Rod. We built a home in New Hope, where we raised our family.

We have three children, five grandchildren, and three great-grandchildren. We also have several step-grands. During our years in New Hope, I returned to work getting a job at Carlson Companies and worked there for nearly 25 years.

After we retired, we traveled extensively both in the U.S. and Europe. Earlier this year, we moved into an Applewood Pointe co-op along the Mississippi and are enjoying retirement, new friends, and the beautiful views.

Mary (Marge) Smith

PATTI AND MARGE

I was born in Nebraska in 1924, the oldest of three. When my sister was an infant, our family moved to Wisconsin, where we grew up. Our brother was born there. He and I survive.

In 1942, I enrolled at Milwaukee State Teachers College. During my freshman year, I decided not to pursue a teaching career. I found my niche in customer service in the Bell System.

During World War Two, I married my high school sweetheart, Roy Smith. He completed his education on the G.I. Bill, graduating from the University of Wisconsin in 1949.

His career with the Joseph Schlitz Brewing Co. took us to Oklahoma, Utah, Texas, and eventually to the Minneapolis area.

Martha, our oldest daughter, was born in Wisconsin. Our son, Charles, was born in Oklahoma, and our twin daughters, Pam and Peggy, in Utah. We met Patti during our second stint in Oklahoma. She became part of our family after our move to Minnesota.

As empty-nesters, Roy and I chose townhouse living in Maple Grove. We enjoyed travel, and we were free to leave with no concerns for outdoor maintenance.

Roy was the grandfather of eight when he passed away in 1991. Since then, I have become a great-grandma to twelve. Chuck died in 2014, leaving my girls and me a family of five.

John Strahan

I was born on December 10, 1937, in Grand Rapids, Michigan, as the first of a pair of twins. In addition to my twin sister, I also had an older and a younger brother. In early 1941 we moved to Detroit to live with my maternal grandparents. During the years of World War II, we lived in a small town near Grand Rapids, where my grandmother had been raised. After the war, we returned to Detroit, and my mother bought a house. I graduated from Cooley High School in 1955 and North Central College in Naperville, Illinois in 1960. I majored in Philosophy and Religion. Being ripe for the draft, I enlisted in the Air Force and served in California for two years in Nevada for one year and in Germany for nearly three years. This is where a German Girl entered our life. I married Barbara Miller of Osseo, Minnesota on August 11, 1962.

Following my discharge in October 1966, we went to Minnesota to start a new life. I got a job with Vincent Brass and Aluminum in December and worked for them for 26 years and two months. I worked in Minneapolis, Cedar Rapids, Iowa, Charlotte, North Carolina, and Minneapolis again. I retired in 1993 when I was 55 years old. I operated a travel business until 2001 and worked at other places after that for a few more years. Barbara retired in 2006, so we could take a 6-week tour to Europe.

We like to travel, and I like to write, especially about family history. One of my goals was to be retired for more years than I had worked for the company. I am ahead by nine months and still counting. A sense of humor helps through rough times of health issues. I can deal with today and plan for tomorrow. The past is behind me. Still looking ahead!

E. Irene Theis

E. Irene Theis is 93 years young and lives in Maple Grove, MN. Irene has long been active in Health Issues, especially women's health. After retiring from Midwest Federal Savings and Loan, she lived up north in the country for over 20 years, gardening, researching, giving seminars, and writing. Since moving back to the Twin Cities area in 2010, her mission is to help others become healthy and to complete and publish her books. The last chapter was about her 90th birthday and her trip to Norway to research family and Malvik Church History.

Leif Wallin

Leif Wallin lives in Minneapolis. Married with two kids, he recently became an empty nester. He retired from a corporate position and now works part-time in the public schools. And he always carries a notebook so he can capture the next piece of a good story.

Carolyn Wilhelm

Carolyn Wilhelm has a BS in Elementary Education, an MS in Gifted Education, and an MA in Curriculum and Instruction K-12. Retired, she now volunteers at an elementary school. Carolyn is a wife, mom, and grandmother. One of her now-adult children was adopted from South Korea.

Recently, Carolyn and her daughter Betsy wrote *A Mom: What is an Adoptive Mother?* Her other self-published children's picture books include the following: *Alex Asks About Auntie's Airplane Day: An Adoption Day Story, Super Spoons to the Rescue; A Math Measuring Story*, and *The Frogs Buy A New House: An Economics Story for Children.*

David Zander

Cultural Anthropologist (Retired)

Member of Story Arts of Minnesota

CAPM lifetime service awardee 2013

Recipient of MN Humanities Center Story Circle grant 2013

Currently collecting Lao and Karen folktales

David Zander is a Cultural Anthropologist who has worked with and written about many of the Asian Pacific refugees and immigrants in Minnesota. The Minnesota History Center has published and archived eight of his life histories of Hawaiians Samoans and Karen in Minnesota. He has published three small collections of Lao,

Karen, and Cambodian (Khmer) folktales and personal stories told by refugees and monks in Minnesota published with the help of graphic design students from Dunwoody College. He has articles published in Asian American Press about Karen monks and was awarded a prize for his article the other face of Bhutan about Hindu refugees from Bhutan who fled to Nepal.

God's Reason

Author Unknown

I don't know how to say it,
But somehow it seems to me
That maybe we are stationed,
Where God wants us to be;
That little place we're filling
is the reason for our birth
And just to do the work we do,
He sent us down to earth.
If God had wanted otherwise,
I reckon He'd have made
Each one of us a little different,
Of a worse or better grade;
And since God knows and understands
All things of land and sea,
I fancy that He placed us here,
Just where He wanted us to be.
Sometimes we get to thinking,
As our labors we review,
That we should like a higher place
With greater things to do;
But we come to the conclusion,
When the envying is stilled,
That the post to which God sent us
Is the post He wanted filled.
And there isn't any service we can scorn
For it may be just the reason
God allowed us to be born.

Thank you for Reading!

We are so happy we could share these stories with you. We hope you will share our book with others it may help.

Footnotes for A Short History of Orphan Trains

1. Social Welfare History Project. (2019). *Orphan Trains.* [online] Available at: https://socialwelfare.library.vcu.edu/programs/child -welfarechild-labor/orphan-trains [Accessed 29 Oct. 2019].

2. Orphantraindepot.org. (2019). History | National Orphan Train Complex. [online] Available at: https://orphantraindepot.org/history/ [Accessed 29 Oct. 2019].

3. En.m.wikipedia.org. (2019). Compulsory public education in the United States. [online] Available at: https://en.m.wikipedia.org/wiki/Compulsory_public _education_in_the_United_States [Accessed 29 Oct. 2019].

4. Childrensaidnyc.org. (2019). A History of Innovation | Children's Aid. [online] Available at: https://www.childrensaidnyc.org/about/history-innovation [Accessed 29 Oct. 2019].

5. HISTORY. (2019). 'Orphan Trains' Brought Homeless NYC Children to Work on Farms Out West. [online] Available at: https://www.history.com/news/orphan-trains-childrens-aid-society [Accessed 29 Oct. 2019

6. The New York Foundling. (2019). History - The New York Foundling. [online] Available at: https://www.nyfoundling.org/who-we-are/history/ [Accessed 29 Oct. 2019].

7. Orphantraindepot.org. (2019). History | National Orphan Train Complex. [online] Available at: https://orphantraindepot.org/history/ [Accessed 29 Oct. 2019].

Made in the USA
Middletown, DE
29 February 2020

85391742R00117